LONDON KLEINIANS IN LOS ANGELES

Also edited by Jennifer Langham

Contemporary Object Relations in Los Angeles:
Building on the Work of the London Kleinians

LONDON KLEINIANS
IN LOS ANGELES
Laying the Foundations of Object Relations Theory and Practice

Edited by

Jennifer Langham

PHOENIX
PUBLISHING HOUSE
firing the mind

First published in 2023 by
Phoenix Publishing House Ltd
62 Bucknell Road
Bicester
Oxfordshire OX26 2DS

Published with the support of the American Psychoanalytic Foundation

British Library Cataloguing in Publication Data

A C.I.P. for this book is available from the British Library

ISBN-13: 978-1-800131-65-1

Typeset by Medlar Publishing Solutions Pvt Ltd, India

www.firingthemind.com

To the memory of

ALBERT MASON

with gratitude

Contents

Part II
Selected papers by founding members
of The Psychoanalytic Center of California

Acknowledgements

Jennifer Langham

We at The Psychoanalytic Center of California are indebted to all of the London Kleinians of the 1960s and 1970s who crossed the Atlantic to lecture on British object relations and to the young analysts who had the curiosity, the creativity, and the courage to arrange those visits. We also owe special thanks to the founding fathers of The Psychoanalytic Center of California and to today's members and candidates who carry our tradition forward.

I am personally very grateful to my friend and colleague Gerald Bernardi for his help in transcribing the lectures that appear in Part I of this volume and to Ebony Towner for her technical assistance and ongoing support. My thanks are due to the *International Journal of Psychoanalysis* for permission to reprint Projective Identification in the Therapeutic Process (Chapter 6) and Bion and Binocular Vision (Chapter 8) and to Nicola Bion Vick and the estate of W. R. Bion for allowing the publication of Notes on Psychoanalysis (Chapter 2) and Some Problems of Observation in Treatment (Chapter 3). Thanks go also to Angela Rosenfeld, executor for the work of Herbert Rosenfeld, for permission to publish Notes on the Diagnosis and Psychoanalytic Treatment of Borderline Patients (Chapter 4), to John Steiner and the estate of Hanna Segal for permission to publish Kleinian Technique (Chapter 1), and to Meg Harris Williams for her permission to include Meltzer's On Autism (Chapter 5) in this volume. Finally, my gratitude extends to Phoenix Publishing House, particularly Kate Pearce, for their trust and encouragement in the development of this project.

About the editor and contributors

Wilfred Bion is one of the most innovative and influential psychoanalytic thinkers of the twentieth century. After acquiring a degree in history at Oxford, he studied medicine at University College London and spent seven years at the Tavistock Clinic training in psychoanalytic psychotherapy. He soon became chairman of the executive committee of the Tavistock Clinic and director of the London Clinic of Psychoanalysis, completed a psychoanalytic training, and eventually became president of the British Psychoanalytical Society. Bion wrote what many consider to be the most important body of work on psychoanalysis after Freud and Klein. In addition to his many published papers, he is particularly noted for the following volumes: *Experiences in Groups, Learning from Experience, Elements of Psycho-Analysis, Transformations, and Second Thoughts.*

James A. Gooch was a training and supervising analyst and senior faculty member at The Psychoanalytic Center of California (PCC) and the New Center for Psychoanalysis in Los Angeles. He was pivotal in the establishment of PCC, having been its founding president. He was also a founding member of the Confederation of Independent Psychoanalytic Societies in the US and served for eight years as the North American Representative to the Board of the International Psychoanalytical Association. Dr Gooch taught nationally and internationally and held the positions of assistant medical director, director of education and research, and chief psychoanalyst at the Reiss-Davis Child Study Center for many years. He maintained a private practice in Beverly Hills with children, adolescents, and adults.

James S. Grotstein was a training and supervising analyst and senior faculty member at the New Center for Psychoanalysis and The Psychoanalytic Center of California in Los Angeles. He was a member of the editorial board of the *International Journal of Psychoanalysis* and a past North American vice-president of the International Psychoanalytical Association. The author of numerous scholarly papers, he has published many books including *Who Is the Dreamer Who Dreams the Dream: A Study of Psychic Presences*, *A Beam of Intense Darkness: Wilfred Bion's Legacy to Psychoanalysis*, and the two-volume work *… But at the Same Time and on Another Level …*.

Jennifer Langham is president of The Psychoanalytic Center of California (PCC), where she is a training and supervising analyst. As a senior faculty member at PCC, she teaches courses in Kleinian theory and technique in the Core Training Program and the Psychoanalytic Psychotherapy Program. Having come to the world of psychoanalysis from a career as a professional cellist, Dr Langham also serves as clinical consultant to the Colburn School Conservatory of Music in downtown Los Angeles. She maintains a private practice in Beverly Hills with adults, couples, and adolescents and has a specialty in treating the performing artist.

Arthur Malin completed medical school at Columbia University, his psychiatric residency at the Los Angeles Brentwood Veteran's Hospital, and his psychoanalytic training at the Los Angeles Psychoanalytic Society and Institute. He was a clinical professor of psychiatry at the UCLA School of Medicine and a training and supervising analyst at the New Center of Psychoanalysis and the Institute for Contemporary

Psychoanalysis in Los Angeles. He was a member of Heinz Kohut's original study group in self psychology and served on the Beverly Hills Board of Education as well. Dr Malin also published numerous articles and chapters on self psychology.

Barnet D. Malin is a training and supervising analyst and senior faculty member at The Psychoanalytic Center of California and the New Center for Psychoanalysis in Los Angeles. He is an associate professor of psychiatry and bio-behavioural sciences at UCLA. Dr Malin teaches extensively in all of these organisations and has lectured nationally and internationally for both psychoanalytic and psychiatric programmes. He has authored several clinical papers and co-edited *Wilfred Bion: Los Angeles Seminars and Supervision* with Joseph Aguayo. His new book, *Questioning Bion's O Concept*, will be published by Routledge.

Albert Mason trained at the British Institute of Psychoanalysis and practised in London before emigrating to the United States in 1969 with Wilfred Bion and Susanna Isaacs to further the work of Melanie Klein. Dr Mason was a clinical professor of psychiatry at the University of Southern California and a training and supervising analyst at The Psychoanalytic Center of California (PCC) and the New Center for Psychoanalysis in Los Angeles. He published and taught extensively in the US and abroad and was a founding member and twice president of PCC as well as a past member of the House of Delegates of the International Psychoanalytical Association. Dr Mason maintained a private practice in Beverly Hills for nearly fifty years.

Donald Meltzer was born in the United States where he completed medical school and his psychiatric training before emigrating to London to pursue his interest in the work of Melanie Klein. He trained as both a child and adult analyst at the British Psychoanalytical Society, where he later became a training analyst and supervisor. His psychoanalytic writings are extensive and highly influential; his writings on the treatment of autistic children are considered especially valuable. Notable among his publications are *The Psychoanalytical Process, Explorations in Autism, The Kleinian Development, The Claustrum, The Apprehension of Beauty,* and *Sincerity and Other Works.*

Of German origin, **Herbert Rosenfeld** attended medical school in Munich and came to England in 1935 to escape Nazi persecution. In London he requalified as a psychiatrist, went into analysis with Melanie Klein, and later completed his analytic training at the British Psychoanalytical Society. He was most noted for his treatment of psychosis using Kleinian concepts, for his groundbreaking work on the destructive aspects of narcissism, and his contributions to the understanding of projective identification. Of particular interest are his volumes *Impasse and Interpretation* and *Psychotic States*.

Polish-born **Hanna Segal** studied medicine in Warsaw and Paris before completing her training at the Polish School of Medicine at the University of Edinburgh. She became one of the most significant figures in British psychoanalysis, known particularly for her ability to clarify and extend the work of Melanie Klein. She qualified as both a child and an adult psychoanalyst at the British Psychoanalytical Society and has published numerous papers and books including *An Introduction to the Work of Melanie Klein*; a biography of Melanie Klein entitled *Klein; The Work of Hanna Segal; Dream, Phantasy and Art; Psychoanalysis, Literature and War*; and *Yesterday, Today, and Tomorrow*. She twice served as president of the British Psychoanalytical Society and as vice president of the International Psychoanalytical Association.

Frederick Vaquer has served as president of both The Psychoanalytic Center of California (PCC) and the New Center for Psychoanalysis. He was a founding member of PCC as well as a founding member of the Confederation of Independent Psychoanalytic Societies in the US. As a senior faculty member and a training and supervising analyst, Dr Vaquer has taught extensively at both Los Angeles institutes and was for many years chairman of the Ethics and Wellness Committee at The Psychoanalytic Center of California where he is now a member emeritus.

Introduction

Frederick Vaquer and Jennifer Langham

Sigmund Freud had little patience with those who put forth what were held to be psychoanalytic ideas, theories, and practices with which he disagreed; Alfred Adler and Carl Jung were prominent examples of those he expelled from the ranks of his early circle of supporters. Although Freud did not openly dismiss the theories and practices of Melanie Klein, her ideas were vehemently attacked and rejected by his daughter Anna. In the early 1940s, Klein and Anna Freud engaged in a series of Special Scientific Meetings organised by the British Psychoanalytical Society to debate the controversies generated by the theories and clinical practice of Klein and to determine to what extent her work deviated from Freud's basic concepts. The outcome of these "Controversial Discussions" was a reorganisation of the British training institute (the Institute of Psychoanalysis) to reflect three differing perspectives represented by the Klein group, the Middle or Independent group, and the Anna Freud group, which carried on the tradition of the classic Freudians.

In the United States, psychoanalysis has traditionally been represented chiefly by classical and ego psychological theories and practices. At one point the American Psychoanalytic Association ejected members espousing what it considered to be dissident notions. Harry Stack Sullivan and Karen Horney were two of the more prominent targets of this expulsive tendency, while Kleinian and British object relations schools of thought were relatively ignored, as few clinicians held them to be of value.

The Los Angeles Psychoanalytic Study Group, established in 1935, became the first psychoanalytic organisation on the West Coast. Later known as the Los Angeles Psychoanalytic Society and Institute (LAPSI), it became the clinical home of many Viennese and German émigré analysts. Disputes between the American medical analysts and the predominantly European lay analysts were among the many complex factors that precipitated a split in the Society in 1950. The new group called itself the Society for Psychoanalytic Medicine of Southern California, clearly distancing itself from LAPSI and clearly leaving the lay analysts behind. In the early 1960s the remaining members of LAPSI were again polarised, due this time to an ideological and personal rift that developed between the supporters of two prominent psychoanalytic figures, Leo Rangell and Ralph Greenson. The two groups actively worked against each other, producing an atmosphere of deep distrust and animosity. It has been suggested that the chaotic and paranoid atmosphere at LAPSI during the 1950s and 1960s provided a generally hostile environment for the arrival of the London Kleinians who eventually settled in Los Angeles.

In the early Sixties a group of young analysts, recent graduates of the Los Angeles Psychoanalytic Society and Institute, formed study groups examining the theories of Melanie Klein and Wilfred Bion; most active in these endeavours were Bernard Bail, Marvin Berenson, James Grotstein, Arthur Malin, and Bernard Branchaft. Subsequently a continuous stream of London Kleinians was invited to lecture, supervise, and settle in the Los Angeles area. Accepting the invitation, Wilfred Bion and Albert Mason emigrated from England in the late 1960s and established practices in Beverly Hills. They were soon joined by Susanna Isaacs Elmhirst. Highly qualified as an MD and training analyst in the British Institute of Psychoanalysis, she had worked for eleven years as physician-in-charge of the Child Psychiatry Department at London's Paddington Green Children's Hospital, where she had succeeded Donald Winnicott. However, she was refused LAPSI membership on the basis of her Kleinian orientation and ultimately returned to London.

Mason quickly became the leading spokesperson for the Kleinian group and, as such, became the centre of a backlash led by Anna Freud with the help of Ralph Greenson. Miss Freud sent a plea to the local analytic establishment demanding the elimination of what she characterised as a metastasis of destructive Kleinian ideas brought to the United States, and Greenson was only too eager to help. The resulting hostility within LAPSI culminated in a formal complaint against the interlopers lodged with the International Psychoanalytical Association. Nevertheless, the ideas of Klein, Bion, and other British object relations theorists gradually took hold.

Since the early 1970s psychoanalysts from the British Psychoanalytical Society have been invited to Los Angeles on a regular basis to lecture and to supervise, thereby contributing to the development of object relations theory and practice in the psychoanalytic community. Part I of this volume contains transcriptions of some of these early lectures, and Part II contains seminal papers written by some of the founding members of The Psychoanalytic Center of California (PCC) before and after its formation in 1984. Today PCC continues to function as a vital centre of psychoanalytic training and education in the British object relations tradition.

Foreword

Barnet D. Malin

At 7:30 one evening, sometime in the mid-1960s, my brother and I were ready to say goodnight to our father, Arthur Malin. He was in yet another of those seemingly endless series of evening meetings, but luckily it was his turn to host it at our home. We stood outside the closed door as Mom tapped lightly and poked her head inside. She motioned for us to go in.

We'd encountered such evening psychoanalytic seminars at our home before. As usual, there were about ten people, some smoking cigarettes, and everyone looking very intent and very serious. But this evening the group seemed a bit perturbed by our intrusion. You'd think it was a primal scene enactment or something. What caught our eyes immediately was the most unusual sight of an older, stout woman with greying hair, settled into a chair, smoking … a cigar. A small one, but a cigar, nonetheless. This was extraordinary. We stared at her in amazement as Dad motioned for us to come over. "Dr Segal, I'd like to introduce my boys, Barney and Norman." She said something like, "It's a pleasure to meet you," in a voice that was just as surprising as her appearance, which now included cigar smoke wafting from her mouth.

She had this wonderful English accent and spoke in a low, grumbly voice that sounded both tough and inviting at the same time.

Dr Segal asked our names, which we repeated politely. She smiled and then asked us, "Do you like James Bond?" We nodded vigorously, and she responded, "Well then, I have something for you." We approached as she reached into her bag to pull out two small metal toy cars. They were gold-coloured Aston Martins, just like James Bond drove. We were absolutely delighted. Dr Segal showed us their special features—press one button and a bullet shield comes up behind the rear window, press another button and groovy machine guns pop out at the front and, best yet, press another button and the top springs open and a little plastic driver goes flying out from the ejector seat. This was fantastic! We thanked her profusely and hoped we could stick around a bit more. I'm sure that Dad's friend, Dr Grotstein, made some sort of joke; I wish I could remember it. But we got the message that it was time to go, because Dad wiggled his eyebrows up-and-down in a not-too-subtle manner. We thanked Dr Segal once more and made our way out. Naturally we began playing immediately with our new James Bond Aston Martin cars (made by Corgi, model 261, the James Bond Aston Martin DB5).

Sometime after Hanna Segal's visit, I was again outside the family room where a meeting was taking place. But this meeting was different. The door was open rather than closed, and it was very, very noisy in there. I walked in to say hello to everyone. There were perhaps eight people sitting around the massive circular main table. Once again there were cigarettes, with alcohol newly added to the mix, and once again there was someone smoking a cigar. This time the smoker was Ralph Greenson (Romy to his friends), who comported himself as the major-domo of the group. Voices, laughter, and spirits were high. It was the monthly poker game; I waved hello to the very important people seated at the table and, as a beginning player, stayed to watch. After a few minutes my father rose and beckoned me back towards the door. "What's wrong?" I asked. He replied, "Barney, you know this is a group of psychoanalysts playing poker here. They are all watching your face, and you are giving their hands away." I burst out laughing and left.

Psychoanalysis in Los Angeles was volatile, political, occasionally corrupt, and always brimming with intensity during the 1950s and 1960s.

Much lay hidden under the rocks of local psychoanalytic societies and institutes. At the Los Angeles Psychoanalytic Society and Institute (LAPSI) Leo Rangell and Ralph Greenson wrestled for power and dominance, practically forcing analysts there to select one camp or another, almost as if to pledge fealty to a tribal leader. Independent thinking was indeed difficult although some, like Ivan McGuire, held their personal ground. Arthur Malin, James Grotstein, and others had personal analyses with McGuire who was very interested in Fairbairn's work and more than familiar with British psychoanalysis. Soon Bernard Bail, Marvin Berenson, James Grotstein, and Arthur Malin—a group whom Grotstein would come to call the Four Horsemen of the Apocalypse— teamed up with another local analyst, Bernard Brandchaft, and began inviting Kleinian analysts from London to sunny southern California for wonderful sojourns presenting to their private study group (that was the apocalypse). This was how Hanna Segal ended up in our family room. The group also brought Herbert Rosenfeld, Donald Meltzer, and Albert Mason to give seminars.

Wilfred Bion moved permanently to Los Angeles in 1968, followed a month later by his young London colleague, Albert Mason. British Kleinian Susanna Isaacs Elmhirst soon joined them and lived and worked in Los Angeles during the mid-1970s. Mason became, unquestionably, the central figure of Kleinian psychoanalysis in Los Angeles, and some might say in the United States. He taught tirelessly, analysed and supervised hundreds of clinicians, gave countless lectures and seminars both there and abroad, and helped establish the Confederation of Independent Psychoanalytic Societies in the United States.

In just a matter of years a Kleinian foothold became firmly established in Los Angeles. The ensuing internecine warfare hit more widely, deeply, and destructively than many might have expected, as individuals and even their non-psychoanalyst family members suffered its impact. Psychoanalysis in Los Angeles suffered as well, as history testifies clearly. And yet, after going somewhat underground, British psychoanalysis re-emerged in the form of The Psychoanalytic Center of California (PCC), founded in 1984, and organised initially by James Gooch and others from the Department of Psychoanalysis at the California Graduate Institute (CGI). The rest, as they say, is history, and thankfully it has been a good history. The PCC became, and still remains, a premier independent North American psychoanalytic society and institute, founded on the principles of British psychoanalysis. Its active and vibrant success stands as a testament to the curiosity and passion of those early psychoanalytic explorers at CGI and LAPSI, to the seeds planted by the Kleinian visitors of the 1970s, and in large part to the dedication and effort of Albert Mason over five decades to teach and train analysts in the Kleinian tradition. The contents of these two volumes demonstrate the success of his pursuits and the durability and value of this psychoanalytic training.

I will close with a personal comment about Dr Mason. After finishing medical school, I returned home to Los Angeles to take a residency in internal medicine. I was aware of something called an Oedipus complex and, comforting myself by intending to "work it out in treatment one day", I switched from medicine to psychiatry and began psychoanalytic training in 1984. Things felt very different in psychoanalysis than what I recalled encountering as a child twenty years earlier. The atmosphere at LAPSI felt quiet, leaden, even dead at times. As a first-year candidate I had only six weeks of studying Melanie Klein during all four years of seminars. Luckily, however, these six weeks were taught by Albert Mason. His breadth of knowledge in metapsychology and clinical case examination, along with his extraordinary articulateness and capacity to relay complex ideas clearly, and his ridiculously wonderful sense of humour, captivated me immediately. I still believe I learned more about psychoanalysis in those six weeks than in any other seminar course I took, and my ongoing contact with Dr Mason afterwards helped make me into the psychoanalyst and person I am today. It gives me, therefore, a great sense of personal satisfaction to help introduce these volumes.

Part I

Beginnings: The early lectures

CHAPTER 1

Kleinian technique*

Hanna Segal

Mr Chairman, ladies and gentlemen, I have chosen the topic of technique tonight for two reasons. There is a great deal of interest in the topic of Kleinian technique. And I have found that a number of analysts who have read a great deal of Kleinian literature and are quite familiar with the theoretical concepts tell me they find it difficult to visualise how Kleinian theory works in clinical practice. They often ask me, "How do you actually do it?" Of course, it's very difficult to explain technique and how one actually works with the cases, but I will do my best to give you some ideas—at least about our principles.

I have also found—and that's my second reason for choosing this topic—a great many misconceptions about Kleinian technique. I have found that people think all sorts of things about Kleinian technique which seem to us very peculiar. For instance, I have been asked whether it is true that we only give oral interpretations. In quite good faith, I have

---

* This is a transcription of a lecture delivered by Hanna Segal at the Los Angeles Psychoanalytic Society and Institute (LAPSI) in January, 1966.

been asked if oedipal interpretations have any part to play in Kleinian technique. It seems to me in the introduction I will give you tonight, I can clear up some of these misconceptions.

This psychoanalytic technique is strictly based on Freudian psychoanalytic concepts. To begin with, the formal setting is the same as in classical Freudian analysis. That is, the patient is offered five or six fifty-minute sessions a week, a couch is provided for the patient to lie on, the patient is invited to free associate, and the analyst interprets the associations.

Not only is the formal setting the same as in classical technique, but in all essentials, psychoanalytical principles are strictly adhered to. That is, the role of the analyst, as in classical technique, is confined to interpreting the patient's material. All criticism, advice, encouragement, and reassurance are rigorously avoided. The interpretations are centred on the transference situation and convey absolutely impartially manifestations of positive or negative transference as they appear. There is no bias that in certain situations it is better to interpret positive or to avoid interpreting positive; we interpret the transference as we see it happening, absolutely objectively. In the transference, special attention is paid to the transference onto the analyst of figures from the patient's inner world. I think I'll expand on this a little later.

The level at which the interpretations are given—again, I think as indicated in various writings by Freud—is determined by what we think is the level of the patient's maximum unconscious anxiety. In this respect, therefore, the Kleinian analyst may be considered to be following the classical technique with the greatest exactitude, in my experience, more so than most other Freudian analysts who find that they have to alter their analytical technique under certain circumstances, as when dealing with pre-psychotic patients, with psychotic patients, with delinquent patients, sometimes with adolescent patients, and with psychopathic patients. There is a long list of sort of special cases in which most non-Kleinian analysts don't adhere to those principles of the classical technique, but use various parameters. Whereas analysts using a Kleinian approach find it usually possible and always desirable to retain the strictly psychoanalytical technique and attitude even with those patients.

Could it be said therefore that there is no room for the term "Kleinian technique" if it is so orthodox in most of its aspects? It seems to me that it is legitimate to speak of the technique as developed by Melanie Klein in that the nature of the interpretations given to the patient and the changes of emphasis in the analytical process show, in fact, a departure or an evolution from the classical technique. Melanie Klein saw aspects of the material not seen before, and interpreting those aspects revealed further material which might not have been reached otherwise and which, in turn, dictated other interpretations seldom used in the classical technique.

I think to understand the rationale of the Kleinian approach, and to appreciate the way in which the technique grew, one has to place it in its historical setting. When Melanie Klein in the twenties started her work with children, she assumed that Freud's analytical methods could be applied to children with only such modifications as would not alter the essence of the psychoanalytical relationship and the interpretive process. Since children do not verbalise easily, and play is one of their major means of expression and communication, she provided each child patient with an individual drawer of small and very simple toys and play materials and proceeded to interpret their play as communication in the way that she would interpret adult patients' free associations, refraining from either educational or other interference. She observed that under those analytical conditions, children develop a transference both positive and negative, often very intensely. She found that the children's communication through various activities in the session revealed an unconscious conflict with the same and often greater clarity than the material of adult patients.

The analysis of small children—I think the youngest patient, the first patient Klein started with was two and three quarters—the analysis of those children fully confirmed all Freud's deductions from adulthood to childhood about the children's sexuality and conflicts, but as might be expected working directly with the child, certain new facts emerged. For instance, Melanie Klein was surprised to see that the Oedipus complex and the superego seemed to be way in evidence at a date earlier than one would have expected, and that both had pre-genital as well as genital forms. Indeed, in analysing small children it seemed to her that the roots of the oedipal situation seemed to reach as far back as the second oral stage.

The superego of the small child wasn't weak or unformed as one would have expected from the assumption that the superego is formed as the heir of the Oedipus complex somewhere in late childhood, but it seems, on the contrary, that the superego of the small child was very well in evidence and possessed very savage primitive oral, anal, and genital characteristics. Far from being weak, the younger and more disturbed the child, the more savage, the more active, and the more in evidence was the child's superego.

Klein was also impressed by the prevalence and power of mechanisms of projection and introjection, the introjections leading to the building of a very complex inner world and the projections colouring all the child's perceptions of reality. Splitting was very active; and the early mechanisms preceding depression and the child's development appear to be a constant struggle towards integration and the overcoming of very powerful splitting mechanisms.

Now, having seen the child when those patterns emerge, one could observe them more easily in the material of adult patients. It is well known that if one recognises a pattern when it is very well in evidence, one can recognise it more easily when it occurs in other circumstances. Working at this primitive level of the child's inner world led Melanie Klein to broaden the concept of unconscious phantasy. So it seems to me that it is impossible to speak about technique without introducing some theoretical concepts, since technique and theory are of course interrelated. I have to apologise here for any repetition to those people who have attended my seminars and also to those who have read much Kleinian literature.

The way in which Melanie Klein broadened and developed the concept of phantasy has been elaborated and set out theoretically in the fundamental paper of Susan Isaacs called, I think, "The nature and function of phantasy". Now, as Strachey remarks in one of his introductory chapters to the new edition of Freud, Freud describes instincts in two different ways which are not quite identical and which he never, as it were, contrasted and elaborated. One of his formulations is that instincts are the psychic representative of biological forces. But another formulation—and it is the second formulation that predominated in his later writings, though he comes back to the earlier one occasionally—but the other formulation is that instincts are comprised of both biological and psychological forces and can only be psychologically apprehended by their psychic representatives. He says that an instinct cannot be experienced or apprehended other than by the psychic representative.

Melanie Klein and Susan Isaacs took the view that the original primitive phantasy is a psychic representative and mental correlate of an instinct. They found that one could expound this view of Freud's that the instinct can only manifest itself by psychic representation to include phantasy as the sort of primary psychic representative of the instinct. Let's say we think of the earliest oral components. The desire to devour corresponding to the phantasy of devouring an object is something that Freud, I think, had in mind in wish fulfilment, early hallucinosis. Then the wish expresses itself by the phantasy of its fulfilment. And on the other hand, the expression of destructive impulses will also be by phantasies. The desire to destroy would correspond to an immediate omnipotent phantasy of destroying and having a destroyed object. In the Kleinian view, phantasy is as old as instinct.

This broader concept of phantasy also provides a link between the concept of instinct and that of ego mechanism. Susan Isaacs, referring to various writings of Freud, has pointed out that what Freud calls the language of the oral impulse, he also calls the mental expression of instincts; that is, phantasies which are psychic representatives of body aims. In an actual example—she speaks of an example of a child's phantasies—Freud shows us that phantasies are the mental equivalent of an instinct, but he's at the same time formulating the subjective aspect of the mechanism of introjection. That is, the phantasy is the link between the id impulse and the ego mechanism—the means by which the one is transmuted into the other. I want to eat, and therefore I have eaten is a phantasy which turns an id impulse into psychic life. But it is at the same time the subjective experience of the mechanism of introjection. When one thinks of a phantasy, one can think of it at the same time as being the expression of the impulse, but also a mental mechanism. This applies to all mental mechanisms, even when they are specifically used as a defence.

We are all familiar, of course, with phantasy as a function of defence. It is a flight from reality and a defence against frustration. This seems contradictory to the concept of phantasy as an expression of instinct, but this contradiction is more apparent than real since phantasy aims at fulfilling instinctual striving in the absence of reality satisfaction. That function in itself may be seen as a defence against reality. But as mental life becomes more complicated, phantasy can be used as a defence in various situations. For instance, phantasies may defend against phantasies in which there is a set of manic phantasies that are used as a defence against underlying aggressive phantasies.

It is Susan Isaacs's contention that what we call mechanisms is an abstract description from the observer's point of view of what subjectively is the functioning of the phantasy. For instance, when we think of splitting, we can describe it as a mechanism, but what the patient is actually doing is living through a phantasy of actually splitting something, dividing something. Probably you're all familiar with patients who bring material about their experience of repression, the phantasies they have about building dams inside, and the anxiety that the dam will break. It's all what we excitedly call mechanisms, and when we come to analyse it, it is an aspect of phantasy.

Now, it seems to me that I have expanded on the understanding of Melanie Klein's use of the concept of phantasy because it is necessary for understanding the technical approach to resistance if we take resistance as synonymous with defences, particularly defences against insight. For instance, a criticism has been levelled that the Kleinian analyst interprets the content of the unconscious and neglects the analysis of defences. This criticism is, I think, based on a misunderstanding of our way of handling defences. It is true that we attach great importance to analysing the unconscious anxiety that is defended against in conjunction with the analysis of the defences against it, so that the emergence of the defended material in consciousness is facilitated not only by the analysis of defences but also by the lessening of the unconscious anxiety through the analysis of the content. I think this is particularly important when one reaches the deep psychotic layers of the personality, as otherwise the ego may be flooded by psychotic anxieties.

In the early days of psychoanalysis, it was considered dangerous to analyse pre-psychotics, for instance, in that the analysis of defences could expose a weak ego to a psychotic breakdown. And this anxiety was fully justified. It is safer to analyse pre-psychotics now when we do not analyse predominantly resistance and defences leaving the ego defenceless against the flooding by anxiety, but when we have some understanding of the psychotic phantasies and anxieties which necessitate those defences and can modify them in the analytical process as well as analysing the defences against them.

The concept of mental mechanism as one facet of phantasy life also implies that there is less division between interpretations of defence and those of content, and that the interpretations can deal more readily with the patient's total experience. It often appears—let's say from Kleinian papers—that when we are analysing phantasies, we analyse the id content and not the defences. This is based on a misunderstanding about what we mean by phantasy, because when we say we analyse phantasy it usually means that we analyse both the instinctual content and the defensive functions in the phantasy.

I think the same applies to the interpretations of structure. Susan Isaacs has made a very clear and strong connection between the concepts of instinct, mental mechanisms, and phantasy—phantasy being the link between the instincts and the mental mechanisms. I have extended it further in a recent paper on phantasy connecting phantasy with the ego and superego structure, a connection which, in fact, is completely implied in Susan Isaacs's paper but not explicitly stated. Because if one views the mechanisms of projection and introjection as being based on primitive phantasies of incorporation and ejection, the connection between phantasy and mental structure also becomes immediately apparent. The phantasies of the object which have been introjected into the ego as well as the loss to the ego by phantasies of projective identification affect the structure of the ego and superego.

When Freud described the superego as an internal object in active relationship with the ego and the id, he was accused at one point by academic psychologists of being anthropomorphic—anthropomorphic in the sense that he saw structures in terms of the little man inside the man. But what was he in fact describing? The structure in the ego is surely the end result of phantasies, because it is in phantasy that the child projects some of his own aggression into a parental figure. It is in phantasy that he incorporates this figure—no child actually eats up the parents—and again it is in phantasy that he attributes to those figures the various attitudes and functions.

Now, Melanie Klein has shown that other objects, earlier than the superego described by Freud, are similarly introjected, and a complex internal world is built in phantasy and structuralised. The fact that the structure is partly determined by unconscious phantasy is of paramount importance from the therapeutic point of view—that in the analytical process we have access to these phantasies. Through mobilising them and helping the patient to relive and remodel them in the analytical process, we can affect the actual structure of the ego and the superego and the patient's personality.

The analysis of phantasy affects, as it were, the whole of our technique, in that the patient's material is looked at from a particular angle. For instance, the patient's communications in the session are viewed as containing an element of unconscious phantasy, though they may seem to be concerned with incontrovertibly external factors. For example, a patient may open the session by complaining that it's cold and raining, a perfect reality statement, and then go on to apparently unconnected material. The analyst will not let it pass as a reality remark. He will keep it in his mind as a communication about something in the patient's internal world. He will wonder, is the patient complaining of the analyst's unfriendliness, is he complaining about the intervals between the sessions, cold and raining, and if he is complaining about the interval, did he feel in the interval as an abandoned baby, wet and cold? Or another possibility: does he have a phantasy that in his omnipotent anger and urination he has flooded the world? Of course, none of these interpretations will be given until other material comes and confirms it, but from the very first communication, there is a sort of open mind about the potential content of phantasy within the most realistic statements of the patient.

Now, in the phantasy world of the analysand, the most important figure is the person of the analyst. That is to say that if all communications are seen as containing an element of communicating to the analyst an unconscious phantasy, it is, I think, equivalent to saying that all communications contain an element of transference. Though we may not always interpret it, what we're interested in is teasing out in the patient's material, that part of it that contains the phantasy about the analyst—the transference phantasy. And it seems to me, from what I've seen of the work of my colleagues from various groups, that the analysis of the transference is much more central in Kleinian analysis than either in the classical technique or in many variations of technique.

For instance, our understanding of the central role of the unconscious phantasy in transference already affects the first session. The question is very often asked by students, "Should transference be interpreted in the first session or should one wait until the patient is ready for it, or the until transference is developed?" If the principle is that interpretations should be given at the level of the greatest unconscious anxiety, and you want to establish contact with the patient's unconscious anxiety, it seems obvious to me that in the vast majority of cases a transference interpretation will impose itself. When a sick person comes to an analyst—commits himself to this fantastic undertaking—it would be most surprising to me if this were not the focus of his greatest anxiety at the moment.

One cannot play principles about these things, but I would say that in my own experience I have not met a case in which I did not feel that I had to interpret the transference from the start. A patient coming to an analysis is bound to be full of hopes, fears, and suspicions in relation to the person of the analyst. Very often those are more clearly presented in the first session than later on when the defences are up. Interpreting them has the effect of first lessening the unconscious anxiety and, from the start, focusing the patient's attention on the central role of the transference situation.

These interpretations, of course, have to be formulated in a way which is acceptable and understandable to a patient as yet unfamiliar with analytical technique. To give you a sort of compound example taken from many supervised cases, a very shut-in, obviously frigid woman patient in her first session is silent and expresses some anxiety about how to behave and what to say, then falls silent. The analyst may very well interpret her fear of his getting in touch with her mind. Then, for instance, as I've seen in such cases—recently supervised cases—the patient proceeds to describe her father as a violent man. In one case he was a drunken Irishman, a father who terrifies her. The analyst can then interpret that she hopes the analyst will get in touch with her and understand her but is also frightened that his interpretations will be violent and terrifying and overwhelm her just as she felt about her father.

In this situation, of course, the analyst will detect immediately her fear of being physically raped, which is already clear in the material.

That need not be interpreted in the first session, though with some patients it has to be. Interpretations which are ready-made in her material—the fear of having her mind penetrated, the fear of being influenced, the fear of being overwhelmed—would at some time be more acceptable to the patient. Indeed, unless the analyst makes those interpretations, the patient remains silent. This paranoid fear of the violent phallic attack on her has to be interpreted for the patient to open up at all, otherwise she would never open up. There are those cases of the silent patient or the distraught patient which don't go anywhere.

In relation to that, another question which is very often asked is at what level to interpret. Should the interpretation be superficial to begin? This is something which doesn't concern us very much. We're not concerned with whether things are called deep or superficial. What we are concerned with is the principle of interpreting at the level of which anxiety is present and active. It is by no means so—that the patient presents first genital, call it superficial, then anal, then deep oral material. The patient presents the material at the level at which it occurs to him at the moment. He is not concerned with what is called deep, what is called superficial. For instance, to establish contact with a schizophrenic patient it is usually useful from the start to interpret the most primitive form of projective identification. I remember interpreting in an adolescent schizophrenic that she felt she had put all her sickness and vomit into me the moment she entered the room and as a result made me a very sick and frightening person. Sick was her word.

A little later in the session, I had an opportunity to interpret to her that she was terrified of my talking because she felt that as I was talking, I was putting all the sickness back into her. And it seems to me that those interpretations lessened the paranoid anxiety sufficiently for her to be able to remain in the room and communicate verbally with me later. Even in the minds of the healthy, however, oral and anal anxieties may be very clearly presented in the transference situation in the first session. As I remember, an analytical candidate started the session by declaring his determination that he was going to be qualified in the minimum time—that he was going to pack all of the analysis he could into the shortest possible time. Later in the session he spoke of his digestive troubles and all sorts of problems he had discarding food which his mother objected to. Sometime later in the session he produced material about cows, observing how cows were milked when he was a child and a variety of material of that type which enabled me to interpret to him that he felt that I was like his feeding mother, the cow. His intention was to empty me as quickly and as greedily as possible and leave me as soon as possible; leave me behind having gotten all the food—an interpretation which mobilised a great deal of material.

Of course I am simplifying things here when I speak of phantasy. When we interpret phantasy we are not only concerned with phantasy. Interpreting the phantasy as related to the current reality, how it influences the reality and the reality influences it, how it relates to events in the past and so on; we see all the various interplay between the phantasy and the impact of reality. The intention of Melanie Klein and the people who worked with her was that the consistent analysis of the transference phantasy in this way would enable us to reach the deeper layers of the unconscious and that those deeper layers have to be reached if we are to get at the basic structure of the patient's personality and the introjections and projections at the early level at which structure is being laid down.

Now in the development of psychoanalysis, as in most sciences, there is an interrelation between technical innovation and theoretical concepts—changes in technique revealing new material, this new material leading to new theoretical formulations, and those in turn affecting technique. Again, it is impossible to speak of technique without bringing in theory. As it is probably well known now, Melanie Klein describes two stages of early development, corresponding to Abraham's pre-ambivalent and ambivalent states. She called them respectively the paranoid–schizoid and the depressive position and describes two different types of ego and object relations and the anxieties pertaining to those two stages. In the paranoid–schizoid position the infant has as yet no concept of a whole person. He relates to part objects, particularly the breast. He also experiences his object as split into an ideal one and a very bad one—something we can see in infant observation.

The anxiety at this stage is of a paranoid nature, hence the name paranoid–schizoid position, that is, the anxiety that the bad object and the destructive impulses placed in the object are going to destroy the self and the ideal object. At that stage, the aim of the infant is to acquire, possess, and identify with this ideal object and to project and keep at bay both the bad object and the threatening destructive impulses. Splitting, projections, and introjections are very active at this stage. The analysis of these anxieties and the defences against them plays a very important part in the Kleinian approach to technique. For instance, if the analyst is very idealised he will be tremendously on the lookout for a split-off negative transference. He will also be very watchful for bad figures in the patient's environment as if the bad, split-off part of the analyst and the projection of the patient's own hostility go into those bad figures. An important mechanism involved in the paranoid–schizoid position, which you've all heard a great deal about, is projective identification. In projective identification, a part of the patient's ego is in phantasy projected into the object, controlling and using it, and projecting into it his own characteristics.

Projective identification illustrates perhaps most clearly the connection between instincts, phantasy, and mechanisms of defence. It is a phantasy which is an expression of instinct in that both libidinal and regressive desires can be omnipotently satisfied by the phantasy—by the phantasy of part of the self entering the object, either emptying it clean, or controlling it, or attacking it in anger. That would be the id part of projective identification.

Projective identification is a mechanism of defence in that, like projection, it defends the patient from certain parts of himself which he then projects outside. It is used to defend against the experience of separation and the experience of any unwanted feelings that can be gotten rid of by projective identification. I should like to give here an example of the technique of the difference of interpreting in terms of projection only, or in terms of projective identification. Again, I will use an example from a student's case material.

A student reports a case in which his woman patient, preceding a holiday break, was describing how her children bickered and were jealous of one another and didn't want to let her get away from them. The student interpreted that the children represented herself, jealous about him in relation to the holiday break. That is, he interpreted the projection—the things she doesn't see in herself that she sees in her children—an interpretation which the patient accepted and which didn't make an iota of difference to her behaviour, either to him or to the children. After the supervision, when certain things were shown to him in a very similar situation, he interpreted that the patient felt she had put a jealous and angry part of herself into the children and that she felt that that part of her was controlling and changing her children. Now, that formulation of the interpretation in terms of projective identification—a phantasy of this child part of her being put into and becoming part of her children—has mobilised a great deal of new material about the various subtle, controlling, and manipulative methods of actually putting that part of herself into the children. As this became clear and she could better accept this part of herself, she could really re-experience her own defended, deprived, and jealous feelings in relation to the analyst. One could say that one actually had to fish for this part of her in the children to enable her to experience it again in herself.

A schizophrenic patient whose analysis I supervised stood at the beginning of his treatment with his back to the analyst and the long table between them. He'd walk all the way around the table and stand with his back to her. Now, that patient as a very small child had been sent overseas and separated from his mother. What the analyst interpreted was that the table represented the ocean that separated him from his mother and that now he was turning the tables on her. In turning his back on her, he was the rejecting mother and he was putting into the analyst a desperate, rejected child part of himself. Following that interpretation and using her countertransference feelings, the analyst could interpret in great detail the different kinds of feelings she felt he was projecting into her. To begin with, the patient reacted to those interpretations as a tremendous persecution. The analyst interpreted to him that now he felt that she was forcibly putting this part of him back into him and, moreover, that she was doing it vengefully. Now she was turning the tables on him. Gradually the patient began to reaccept this part of himself and then, as it were, he faced the analyst and started talking to her.

When states of mind of projective identification predominate, the patient may feel depleted through losing parts of himself. He may also feel persecuted by the analyst while the analyst, in turn, is filled by the patient's unwanted part and the experience of wanting to put it back into the patient, who has become confused with the analyst. This is particularly noticeable in the case of the schizophrenic. It is to be emphasised that the analysis of the paranoid–schizoid object relationship and defences is not confined to the analysis of the psychotic and the pre-psychotic only. The schizoid defences, thoughts, and anxieties, though they originate in the early stages of development, are repeatedly regressed to, even in the most normal individual as a regression against later depressive anxieties. I think it's probably quite familiar to you that paranoid anxieties are linked to what we call schizoid defences.

The depressive position starts when the infant begins to recognise his mother as a whole object and has the idea of the object split into a good and a bad one. Indeed, those first integrations happen simultaneously because they're interrelated. As the object becomes integrated, as the mother becomes a whole person, she also becomes recognised as this person who can come and go and is both good and bad. Simultaneously with the parts becoming a whole, the good and bad also become whole. And this integration in the object is, of course, accompanied by the integration in the self. The child gradually comes to realise that it is the same infant, himself, who loves and hates the same person, his mother. He then experiences ambivalence and a new set of anxieties. Whereas previously he was afraid that he would be destroyed by his persecutors, he now dreads that his own aggression will destroy his ambivalently beloved object. His anxiety shifts—in Kleinian terms— from the paranoid to the depressive. And since at that stage the infant's phantasies are felt in a very omnipotent way, he is exposed to the experience that his aggression destroys his mother, leaving him in a state of loss and mourning when so often the absence is experienced as an actual death.

Furthermore, as the depressive position begins in the oral stage of development and the object is constantly being introjected, those ambivalent attacks are not only in relation to the mother as an external object, but to the mother as an internal object as well. The infant experiences depressive anxiety, feeling that in his hatred, he has devoured and destroyed not only his external mother, but also his internal ambivalently loved mother, producing a state of chaos and disintegration in his internal world. There is a difference here between the classical view and the Kleinian view on the relation between mourning and the depressive illness. In Freud's and Abraham's view, the depressive illness is a situation in which the patient is mourning an ambivalently loved and attacked internal object. In Freud's view, normal mourning would include only the loss of the external object, not mourning in relation to an internal object. In the Kleinian view, the depressive position and the depressive anxiety is a normal part of development. In normal mourning those early anxieties are reawakened—that is, the person experiencing a normal mourning would also experience, to begin with, the loss of an internal as well as an external object.

Another technical difference I've often heard is that periods of mourning are sterile periods for the analysis. I've even heard of a case in which the patient was more or less encouraged to stay away from the analysis until he'd gone through the mourning. Only then would the analysis restart. In Kleinian analysis, we find that periods of mourning are extremely important, both because they help the patient work through the mourning, and the mourning can be made use of for analytical purposes. The analyst can use the mourning situation to help the patient reintegrate, relive, and give up his internal object.

The intensity of the pain and anxiety in the depressive position, even in normal development, mobilises a powerful set of defences which we call the manic defences. These manic defences involve some regression to earlier schizoid mechanisms like splitting, denial, idealisation, and projection—basically schizoid mechanisms. The important thing about the manic defences is that they form a sort of mob-like organisation defending the ego against the experience of depressive anxiety. Since depressive anxiety arises out of the infant's recognition of the mother as a whole object on whom he depends, and in relation to whom he experiences ambivalence and the subsequent fear of loss, this whole relation has to be denied. Denial of the importance of the object, triumph over it, control, contempt, and devaluation are all object attitudes which defend the ego against the experience of valuation of the object, dependence, and ambivalence with its concomitant depressive anxieties. For instance, a patient following the recognition of his oral attachment to his analyst, his greed for analysis, and his urinary attacks against the analyst had the following two dreams: in the first dream, he saw a house on fire and collapsing, but he drove past it thinking the fire was really of little importance. In the second dream, he stole two buns from a bread shop, but he thought it didn't matter very much since they were such tiny little buns. It was quite clear from the patient's previous material that the two buns were the two breasts reflecting a displaced oral attachment to the analyst, and that the burning house was a reference to previous session material of his very violent urinary attacks which were felt as burning. His anxiety about the fire was dealt with by denial (it's of so very little importance) and the guilt about stealing was defended against by devaluation and contempt (they are such tiny little buns).

Those dreams were very important because the fire was associated in his mind with the burning in his stomach (he had gastric cancer), and the collapsing house was associated with his constant delve into depressive collapse. One could show him how this manic defence was defending him against anxiety (those things were of such little importance), an attitude he often had. One could also show how the defence increased the depressive anxiety because the more he denied the attacks, the more he attacked and had the greatest burning in his stomach. Manic defences by their very nature lead to a vicious circle. The depression is the result of the attack on the original object. The manic defences preclude the ego from the experience of depression, but they also preclude the working through of the depressive position and necessitate a further attack on the object by denial, triumph, and contempt—thereby increasing the underlying depression.

It is well known that where there are manic phenomena, one has to look for the underlying depression that is defended against. It is also well known and equally important that where there is a depressive presenting illness, there is an unconscious manic mechanism of defence which precludes the working through of the depressive anxiety. The manic defences prevent the patient from working through the depressive position and therefore from mobilising the normal capacity for reparation. If the infant feels that in his hatred he has destroyed his good external and internal object, the experience is a feeling of pining and longing and also a longing to restore what he remembers as this loss of a good internal and external situation. This is a drive which we think underlies a great deal of creativity and sublimation.

It will be clear from the foregoing that technically we attach the greatest importance to the analysis of the manic and schizoid defences to enable the patient to experience depressive anxiety and to work it through by way of restoration of the internal object. We do not consider the paranoid–schizoid and depressive positions merely as stages of development. We consider them to be two types of ego integration: one early and one later. There is, therefore, a constant struggle in the ego to maintain the full depressive level of integration with the constant possibility and threat of the manic defences or the regression to the paranoid–schizoid position.

I haven't got time to go into all the ins and outs of it, but I want to say just one or two things about the Oedipus complex. In Kleinian analysis, as in classical analysis, the Oedipus complex remains very much a central preoccupation. We see the Oedipus complex, to begin with, as starting earlier. I think it is quite implicit in the definition of the depressive position that the Oedipus complex starts there; when the mother becomes a full person, she becomes a person having many relationships. She becomes an object of jealousy as well as envy. If we think of the paranoid–schizoid and the depressive position as two types of ego organisation, it is extremely important how the Oedipus complex is experienced. It can be experienced in a paranoid way, it can be experienced in a depressive way, and it can be defended against in a manic way. There are all sorts of ways in which the depressive and paranoid–schizoid states of mind end up in the structure of the Oedipus complex. I will now take one example from one dream of a patient to try to tease out for you the various elements that you would be interpreting in such an oedipal situation.

The patient had the following dream: he dreamt that he was in a strange place where the wash area was out in the open, so that he had to undress and wash naked. There were other naked people present. He suddenly noticed on a kind of platform a couple facing one another, each pointing at the other an identical lethal weapon. It was like a camera but more bottle shaped, and it was covered by something like a camera hood made out of tin foil. If the tin foil was lifted, a lethal ray of radiation would be released. He was absolutely sick with apprehension knowing what would happen. One of them, probably the woman, lifted the hood, directing the ray at the man. For a moment he thought that at least the other one would not retaliate, that the second death wouldn't set anything right. But of course, as he knew, the man immediately retaliated and the dreamer experienced a sense of utter hopelessness at the senselessness of the destruction. He also felt a considerable anxiety about himself in that he thought he might have been in the field of the rays and feared they might have got into him. These associations started, as you might have guessed, around the nuclear armaments and the problems of retaliation. I won't go into the details, but he had associations about the feelings in the dream. Then he turned to the memories of his sexual curiosity in childhood in association with the wash area and the various times he observed his parents. The camera with the lethal ray he associated with his mother's piercing eyes. That was familiar material related to his experience that his mother used her eyes to control father and him, as well as the feeling, when he was very little, that her eyes could kill. The association that really upset him was the association with the tin foil, because he knew precisely what it was. He kept two bottles of brandy to give as Christmas presents, one to his analyst, and one for his wife's analyst. He was thoroughly shocked as he recognised that in the dream, the couple of bottles that he gave to the analysts appeared to those two analysts the lethal weapons with which they were going to destroy one another.

The dream is clearly concerned with the patient's sexual curiosity about the parents—his oedipal jealousy—but I want to tease out certain elements in it, for our understanding of it may be affected by what we said about the paranoid and depressive states. In addition to analysing his sexual curiosity, emerging at that point from repression, and his jealous feelings in the transference around his curiosity about the analyst's Christmas holiday (does she meet this man who is the wife's analyst?), I think the following elements were taken up in the course of this session and the next. There was a tremendously strong projective element in his enquiries. As he is curious, so the two parents acquire those murderous lethal camera eyes; his omnipotent voyeuristic projection affects his perception of his parents in relation to one another (they kill one another with looks) and in relation to himself (his mother's eyes control him as do the rays).

The introjection of the whole situation is expressed in the dream by the patient's feeling that he's in the field of the rays and that they may fall into him. That is, the parents into whom he projected the bad feeling are re-introjected, and they become very much a part of his hypochondriacal anxiety which is always fairly active in this patient and was particularly active in the day or two preceding this dream. Now the depressive elements, I think, are also very active in this dream, both in his introjection of the parents and in the tremendous pity and concern and anxiety experienced in relation to them. It seems to me that I have to stop at this point.

CHAPTER 2

Notes on psychoanalysis*

Wilfred Bion

I find it somewhat intimidating to be expected to talk about my concepts because I don't think I have any. I think it's a sort of mistake that very easily arises, because I don't think I've ever said anything original in my life. I think that what I say is probably unique simply by definition because we concern ourselves with the individual as being uniquely important. I think it serves to say that psychoanalysts attach enormous importance to the individual person. I don't know if it was ever built into some sort of philosophy or was stated as if it were a philosophical prejudice or a philosophical point of view, but it seems to me that that is just what it is: that we are concerned with unique people and the uniqueness of the person.

Now, this raises a problem because in a sense we are also concerned with the fact that the individual is a member of the human race, to put it at its most vague. That is why it is interesting to consider what Freud regarded as being the hallmark of analysis, which means both the hallmark of the actual procedure and the hallmark of the subject which we

---

*This is a transcription of a lecture delivered by Wilfred Bion at the Los Angeles Psychoanalytic Society and Institute (LAPSI) in 1975.

investigate, which is the human individual. That part of the problem takes up very little of our time, or so it seems to me, because for about three sessions psychoanalytic theory is quite useful because we've got nothing else to go on. One knows virtually nothing about the person concerned, so you have to fall back on theories and expectations which you can entertain from past experiences you've had and from the literature. After that, if the analysis proceeds, you're up against a unique situation. You're up against that unique individual.

John Rickman, whom I first went to for analysis for a long time, used to say that anybody could regard himself as an analyst if he could see a patient for two sessions. He considered that to be a pretty substantial achievement. And I know what he means, because I have seen quite a lot of people once but never again. There are a certain number though, who seem to want to go on with the whole proceeding. And that is where you get into the real problem of *what is psychoanalysis*.

So, I want now to change the subject, rather. In his book on symptoms, inhibitions, and anxieties, Freud says there's much more continuity between intrauterine life and earlier infancy than the impressive caesura of active birth allows us to suppose, to believe. I found that extremely illuminating, because in various ways that peculiar little pattern seems to repeat itself over and over again. That you constantly find that the analysand tells you something, and it seems to have a sort of reminiscence about it. It reminds you of something earlier, or what we call earlier, and indeed the patient—or the analysand—seems to be repeating a sort of reminiscence.

As you know, Freud hit on this scheme by which he discovered that if people associated freely, then these apparently free associations were somehow connected with each other. This point was not, and still is not, obvious. One has to believe that that is true, and the next thing is that you have to believe it enough to go on listening to these free associations until there begins to emerge some sort of connection between them. This brings me to yet another point. One gets an extraordinary amount of material. You get every sort of material, from the patient who talks very freely, very easily, very coherently and articulately, to the patient who will go through a session without saying a word.

Silence isn't what one ordinarily calls free association, but I think one has to consider that it *is* a free association. The fact is that we don't know, and I certainly don't know, and perhaps a matter for future research is: is it possible to make any progress with a patient who doesn't say anything? Then take another kind of patient: the kind of patient who would be quite prepared to play a musical instrument if he thought that the analyst was capable of understanding music but does not feel willing to talk and considers the whole process of talking to be a very feeble and faulty method of investigation or communication, even. I have known a patient who is quite hostile to the idea of verbal communication. Not just in psychoanalysis, but verbal communication in general on the grounds that it is a ridiculous and incompetent method of communication. And I'm reminded at this moment too of the odd fact that people even write differently. If you take a Chinese person, he does not write from left to right. Is there any difference between the person who writes from right to left and the person who writes from the bottom upwards? Could one say they think like that? Certainly, a lot of trouble was caused because, for a long time, an attempt was made to understand Chinese on the grounds it was like any other article of speech. But it isn't. It is pictorial, in origin at any rate, with little drawings, little pictures, although they now have lost their resemblance to what they are fundamentally supposed to represent.

Amongst our patients, I think you get the same thing. The patient says he talks, shall we say, in quite an ordinary manner, just using ordinary articles of speech. Well, it's no good telling him back again what he said. He knows that anyway. What then are we trying to tell him? Or what then is it that we want to draw attention to? Certainly, in analysis itself one does get a sort of feeling that there's something important that the patient is trying to communicate. He doesn't come and waste his time and his money just about nothing, although he very often says so or even wants to make you believe that it is so. So one problem is: what is this pattern which we are trying to detect, or are thinking that we do detect, other than what is communicated by ordinary articulate speech?

One reason I mentioned this statement of Freud's is because it seems to me that there is again a peculiar oddity, a peculiar gap between what the patient is saying in his ordinary articulate speech—his free association—and what we think we would like to communicate if we knew what the interpretation was. He also pointed out that if one left a happy spirited discussion with friends about recently debated topics to get down to the job of arranging introductory lectures on the subject for a large audience, one may be struck by a certain oddity. The two worlds seem to have no connection.

Now that again seems to me to be peculiar and to be reminiscent of this caesura which Freud speaks about—this thing which seems to be the impressive act of birth. Well, there are plenty of these impressive things. The patient will often try to impress the analyst with an impressive fact. It's impossible to say what is bothering him. The difficulty is that one has to be receptive not only of what is said but of what is not said. In the instance of this impressive caesura, the fact is that there is this sort of gap. I don't think it is only a matter of being between prenatal and ante- and post-natal life, but it also has to do with what we are usually quite familiar with as resistances. I'm not at all sure that one won't really have to revise this again as a matter for research which all of us have to concern ourselves with as to the nature of these resistances. Although a great deal has been done and has indeed been formulated, I'm sure there's a great deal more that has to be done to be useful for psychoanalysis. Every solved problem simply opens up vast new areas of unsolved problems.

Let us come back to a very interesting point in the practice of psychoanalysis: the vastness of the material that confronts us. I'm including here the vastness of the experience when it includes silence—or as I suppose musicians might say, rests. Because in the totality of musical compositions at any rate, you also have these silences. They play a very big part in the composition and the understanding of music. I don't think that we can neglect them because they are so important. And in fact, every now and then you get some sort of curious event like the person who, for some obscure reason, doesn't or won't listen to the music but listens to something else. It's like Freud, who doesn't listen to what the person is trying to communicate, but listens to something else, and the next thing you know you've got this vast realm of psychoanalysis.

Our problem is not what to do because we know so little. That will always be with us. The thing is the enormity of what has to be learned, partly because one can never get rid of one's ignorance and partly because the realm of what is not known is terrific. In practice, you are confronted with the problem of choice. It's not a question so much of trying to think up what possible interpretation there is, because there are millions of them, millions of them. It is a question of which one to give in the very limited space of time available. It's a problem of choice. Another problem is getting the objects from which we are going to choose into some kind of order. One wants to decide which of the various alternatives to mention first. Now that involves what one could call non-pathological splitting. After all, one is dealing with whole people, one is dealing with a whole universe. Even if you talk about the universe of discussion—if you put a kind of barrier around what topics you want to talk about—even then, you've got a vast choice and the problem of splitting this total mess into bits by what I call non-pathological splitting. However, I think that all splitting has been non-pathological at some time. The infant and the child cannot really grasp the totality of the world in which they live. The have to split it. They have to split it into different little packets. And as I say, if one could take it in slow motion, one would then have to consider which order to put those packets into and then which one to interpret; which one of them to formulate and what words to formulate it in.

In his discussion of lay analysis—I think I'm right—Freud mentions this fact: that there's the problem of what to teach. Supposing one is concerned with teaching people to be analysts. Even if you take the very little bits that we already know, it involves things like philosophy, science, music, mathematics. You can multiply the list straightaway for yourself faster than I could think of it even. So there again is this problem of choice: how is one to pick out of all that lot the most important things for an aspiring analyst to learn?

It's curious in mathematics that you seem to have more discussion of probability, which seems to me to be very much a discussion of something which analysts would know more about than most people, because one is always concerned with the probable. But there doesn't seem to be much about the mathematics of choice. Or it may simply be that I'm purely ignorant of it. But it is a matter that concerns us very much indeed, and we might be able to throw some light on this or produce some sort of material with which really capable mathematicians might do something. The mathematicians may indeed be able to help us if only they knew a little bit of what we know. Which might be a gain, you see, but it doesn't do for us to suppose that we have no contribution to make. It's very difficult to combine this state of affairs where it's constantly brought home to us how little we know without losing sight of the fact that we know something, and that it might be worth communicating.

Now, it might be worth communicating, but how is one to get across this gap? How is one to get across this caesura? As I say, I don't think we ought to be content in supposing that this is solved, or the problem is a closed problem when one considers the theories of resistance, or any other psychoanalytic theory. One should give due weight, have great respect for what has already been found, but not to the exclusion of what hasn't been found. And this matter of resistance seems to be one of them. This impressive caesura; this impressive resistance which may indeed hide from us as much as it illuminates. How are we to get across that gap? Not simply in this impressive act of birth, but the birth of an idea. Supposing anybody comes across or has an idea, how are they first of all to communicate it to themselves? That would seem to be extremely easy. But from my observation, and I don't know why, it seems to require enormous courage. Patients have ideas. They won't express them—sometimes to the point where a patient will go through session after session entirely silent. But then they do that with themselves. They won't write, or they won't draw, or they won't paint, or they won't try musical composition, because they dare not. Because they dare not communicate to themselves, say, the musical composition because it would sound so horrible if they tried. And they would rather make excuses or reasons for not doing it. Well, one wonders …

Extend that for yourselves. How much are we actually dealing with people who are patients, or call themselves patients, or dare to come to a psychoanalyst, but who really need some sort of assistance which would enable them to penetrate their own resistance, or that would enable them to penetrate whatever seems to get in between themself and themselves. Of course, one does try to draw attention to the fact that they can't communicate with themselves or with the analyst. But, in fact, that is only a transitive experience; an experience which is *in transit*. The purpose of interpreting what Freud described as the transference is really a kind of transitive activity on the way to something else. My own impression is that it's on the way to their being able to communicate with themselves. All this, of course, would be refuted by any non-analyst who would say, "Well, of course anybody likes having an analysis. Who wouldn't? Just talking about themselves; they'd be absorbed with it, and they'd be delighted to do it." Yes, but it isn't so. And we as analysts have good reason to know that it isn't so. In an activity which is supposedly to help patients to talk about themselves—in fact, they seem to find the most intense difficulty in doing so; they seem to hate the process and as likely as not, hate you in the process.

I think I would now like to indulge in a bit of what is probably nonsense—more than usual, I mean. If it is true that there is some sort of mental life in the foetus, what are we to do about that? What are you to do with a patient whom you feel you could go on analysing until the end of time without it making a difference because there seems to be such a gap between themself and themselves that one doesn't seem to be able to penetrate it at all.

Suppose a patient comes and complains that they have headaches or migraines and then, after a time, it turns out that they see what used to be known as fortification patterns. The headaches are accompanied by apparently peculiar images. Does that start after birth—in infancy or childhood? Or could it possibly be one of these things which are antenatal and which nevertheless, as far as symptoms are concerned, penetrate the fact of birth, the caesura. One could go on with this to the point of making it ridiculous and say, "Alright then. When the optic pits are formed, what does the foetus see? When the auditory pits are formed, what does the foetus hear?" But the point would be something of this sort: is it possible to conceive of any psychology as existing before birth, and is it possible that some of what we see and hear in the office is a sort of vestige of something which is antenatal but which is, nevertheless, having a powerful influence much as the unconscious idea influences unconscious behaviour? Could it be possible, for example, that the embryo doesn't see anything? On the other hand, we do know that if we were to apply pressure to our eyeballs, we would see things. One sees lights and so forth. If that is the case, why shouldn't the infant, or the embryo even, be subjected to pressures which translate themselves into sight that is, in fact, produced by pressure, not light?

By analogy, is the conscious patient—the patient we deal with—suffering from a reminiscence which has undergone that sort of transformation? I mention migraine because it's one of these things which is so often regarded as a sort of psychosomatic affair. But one wonders, you see, the extent to which we are dealing with physical events that have been transformed into psychological events. We're in the habit, very often, of talking about past events: "You probably felt such and such when you were an infant or child." Well, that seems to me to be extremely deceptive, because in fact, all that we really know and all that the patient really knows is what they feel now, in the present. But is there some present vestige of a thing which was once conscious, or once current? Because the present in that case is simply the future of a past event. But what we're dealing with is a present event involving the patient—man, woman, or child—who comes to us. Even now, I find this extremely difficult to talk about because I don't think there's a language for it. There may be things for which we have found no language whatever. These things may be residual effects, effects which are due to this continuity which Freud talks about between intrauterine life and earliest infancy.

What we're concerned with is, in what language are we to talk to them? How or what interpretation are you to give to a patient who says that they have a headache, or that they feel physical symptoms. Dream? No. No dream. Which may mean, you see, that they've had no *articulate* dreams. But why on earth does one have an articulate dream? Dreams are pretty fantastic anyway, even when they are articulated, verbalised, and passed on to us. Why shouldn't there be dreams which are purely physical? It doesn't sound particularly important, perhaps, but suppose you have a patient who cannot or won't lie on the couch, and can produce any number of reasons for not doing so, and can even produce in you any number of reasons (or rationalisations, I should prefer to say at this point) of why the patient doesn't lie on the couch.

Now, when you go on giving interpretations with no effect whatsoever, it seems to me that one should consider that one's rational interpretations are really indistinguishable from rationalisations. If that is the case, one has to reconsider altogether the nature of interpretations and what we have to deal with. As I say, one has to consider the possibility that the patient cannot bear the pressure of the couch on his backside, or on his front side, if it comes to that. But this seems to me, again, to be a matter which can only be decided in the consulting room. In a sense, this is the fascination of analysis. One's got to dare to be ignorant and to hope that the patient would also dare to be ignorant. It's such a bore when the patient says, "Yes, I know. Yes, I know. Yes, I know" to everything you say to him. I've a mind to say, "Oh, for heaven's sake, be ignorant," but one can't. It's not one of the interpretations which is in the manual!

There again, you see, is a problem of: do we know what analysts should do or be? One could rapidly get in a state, you see, in which the analyst himself turns into the most extraordinary sort of person who's apparently got no feelings and is apparently able to stand anything. But I'm not sure that isn't really putting forward a very powerful interpretation. The patient can go by what the analyst is saying or doing. And again there's this problem as to what language we are to use. I take refuge in the fact that this is research and therefore, I don't really feel under any particular pressure to answer these questions. But it seems to me to be rather important to try to at least indicate some of the questions that plague me. With a bit of luck, I might even hear an interpretation or two that might come in handy. But the point of it is really the perpetual research, the perpetual fact that in analysis, one is dealing with an open-ended question. The past, what is known, interpretations which are given and so on—these are very rapidly of no importance. The present and the future which hasn't happened yet: that is important. It's also very difficult. For the future which hasn't happened yet is as bad as the past which you can't remember—worse, in fact.

What I feel sometimes is that the attempt to think of it in terms of the past, or infancy and so on, becomes somewhat more of a liability than an asset because it hides the fact that one is dealing with a person (a mind) of character and personality there in front of you. And it's curious, you see, if you start thinking about what the person may feel. While one is thinking about that, time passes, and one is not able to listen to the patient or to observe what is going on. That is why I sometimes put this as getting rid of one's memory or one's desire, because they act as a sort of barrier. Because while you are wondering about the patient's past, the patient's present goes on playing through. Or while you are wondering either about what you are going to do or what the patient's going to do, or what's going to happen to the patient, something *is* happening, and one fails to notice what is happening. Therefore, I don't really think of it in terms of what the patient felt, but rather in terms of there being various levels of the mind, which again is an artefact. I think it's most unlikely that there are levels of the mind—anyhow we couldn't see them or feel them or touch them or anything. It is just a sort of theory or hunch one puts forward to ease oneself; a theory to make the comprehension easier, or at any rate, to make one *feel* that one has understood the patient. And the whole time, there is reality. There are such things as facts, or so we think. One thinks that there is such a thing as character or personality. Either that, or we're simply crazy for spending our lives and time and everything on psychoanalysis. The whole thing is based on the assumption that there is a mind that we're investigating, I think with very good reason. But it does lead to this difficulty about the immediate problem where it seems to me that one could say that the patient is having a feeling because they've got a very long history; it almost certainly existed at birth or before and still does. That's the point. Now whether that's a true description, I've no idea. I think the most that one can hope for, in a sense, is that it might be illuminating. I'm reminded of Bacon's essay. "What is truth?" asked jesting Pilate and wouldn't wait for an answer. Well, we seem to think it's worthwhile waiting for an answer. And Freud suggests that there's a lot to be said for going on watching or listening for a pattern until—whatever the patient may be saying or doing—a pattern emerges.

But of course, many patients are afraid of insanity and are therefore afraid of expressing thoughts or ideas which could be described as irrational and could be nipped in the bud straightaway. Although most patients have had good ideas at varying times, they may have learned that it can be very unwise to do so. We are quite accustomed to the fact that it is just as well that if one can say anything at all, one should at least *sound* rational if one's going to avoid getting locked up somewhere. But somebody's got to dare to be psychotic or crazy or idiotic, or listen to the wrong thing, like people who won't listen to music but listen to the interference. The next thing you know, you've got your radio, telephones, and all the rest of the apparatus doing nothing more than just listening to the interference.

Well, I think that I would like to stop at this point, somewhat arbitrarily, since I know myself well enough to know that I'm fair to talk for as long as my voice lasts. And I don't know that that's a particularly good idea.

Audience member:

It's interesting, Dr Bion, what you say about physical ailments having a possible effect upon the sympathetic or the parasympathetic nervous system. For about two years, I had Dr Arthur Mirski as a consultant on one of my projects. Mirski was trained in psychoanalysis, biochemistry, physiology, and animal behaviour. When Jolly West introduced him at UCLA he said, "We have this professor here, and this professor here, and that professor, and we have one *super-professor*." That was Mirski. Now Mirski had the idea, and he felt he got the idea on a number of occasions, that seems related to one of your far-out ideas; he said that at times there were circumstances when he could, from dream material, describe the area of a person's physical illness, and he said it convincingly.

Dr Bion responds:

Well, I think, like myself, you've all known the case of the really brilliant clinician who will walk into a ward, see a patient, and give a diagnosis when nobody else had been able to diagnose that patient. Nobody else solved the problem of why this particular patient was ill. I remember one instance in which a particularly sensitive clinician was able, although it wasn't his patient, to recognise the disease condition, but I think that was due to being very sensitive to his own sense impressions and the physical facts which were presenting themselves to him.

Now, if that is the case, it seems to me that one could possibly extend all that. One could extend it so that you could get a person who is a psychoanalyst who may nevertheless also be concerned with psychosomatic diseases or possibly drift further and further in the direction of making a psychological approach to physical illnesses. It seems to me, for example—and this raises another point—you say to the patient, "What's the matter?" "Oh, it's my hands, doctor. They're awful. The pain is frightful," and so on, for one hundred thousand cases, saying the same thing to you. Now, I sometimes wonder whether it wouldn't be convenient for an analyst to have ten patients instead of having a hundred thousand or whatever it is. Having ten in a bunch in the hope of all of them saying, "It's my hand, doctor," and so on and so on. It might intensify the phenomenon to a point where it became possible for the analyst to observe what the pattern was.

I'm not suggesting of course that rheumatism is a psychological complaint, but on the other hand, I do suggest that even with physical complaints, people have got a psychology about them. We may be concerned, you see, with the psychology of the patient who is ill or the patient who has got some specific illness. It might also be possible to be concerned with the physical illness making the approach from the mind. Not from the physical to the mind but from the mind to the physical. This incidentally really opens up to another subject—namely direction in analysis. One talks over and over again, you see, with various coordinates in the past or in the future, or in childhood, in infancy, in adolescence—all these terms. But in fact, nobody has ever worked out what the coordinates are of the mind or the personality. That has got to be done sometime.

Audience member:

I have three things I'd like to ask you about or talk to you about. You are always subtle, I realise that, but, as subtle as you are, you stimulate people to think in an unusual way. You make their usual thoughts much more valid to them than they are willing to admit to themselves or to others. So I'm thinking my usual thoughts, but I'm thinking them more intensely than usual. And there are three things you have stimulated me to bring up and discuss with you. One is a phrase you used early in tonight's talk. You said, "As the analysis proceeds." I missed some of the things that you said later, because I was dwelling on that. You said, "As the analysis proceeds." We know, or we should know, or we should spend much time trying to know about the time of an analysis proceeding. When we are asked whether an analysis is proceeding, we say, "Why yes, this is going on and that's going on," or we know something about the signs of an analysis not proceeding. We say such and such and such and such. I find myself wanting to know more about whether there are analyses that proceed in the patient but not in the doctor, analyses that proceed in the doctor but not in the patient, or analyses that proceed in certain parts of each. You talked about various levels. Just using that kind of imagery for a moment, an analysis may be proceeding on some levels and not on other levels—in the doctor, in the patient—but whether there's contact between these levels is difficult to know. But enough about signs. Signs we teach each other about, or we look up in the literature. But what is the essence of an analysis proceeding? What does that really mean, that an analysis proceeds? A derivative question is, can an analysis not proceed? Is there any way possible for an analysis not to proceed, and what is the essence of an analysis not proceeding? Now, there are two other things I'd like to bring up, but should I stop now?

Dr Bion responds:

I was also thinking as Dr Anderson was speaking, and it occurred to me once more, how we are dominated by our eyes and our sight and what we think we see. One of these things is the anatomy or physiology of the other person. Now the question which Dr Anderson raises seems to be: where, in fact, does thinking go on? Can we really rely on the impressive fact of one's own skin and anatomy to assume that one's thinking stops where one's skin stops, or that our methods of communication stop when we stop talking? Our thinking certainly doesn't stop when we stop talking, or when we stop being awake. So this whole question is: what are the boundaries of the mind or the personality or the character, or even of a group of people like ourselves here. In short, one of the real troubles about this is that thinking does go on. The sins committed in the name of psychoanalysis are, as you know now, of a pretty considerable size. There's a pretty considerable crop of ideas which are attributed to psychoanalysis and psychoanalysts, all kinds of methods of treatment to which I don't think that we would subscribe at all, that are nevertheless called psychoanalysis. And this really makes it all pretty difficult. Because even when one comes across a real analyst, one has very little reason to believe that they are a real analyst because real analysts are two a penny if you listen to what people have to say.

You consider what trouble was started by Freud, when he thought of the whole thing. It certainly didn't stop where he stopped. I don't know what can be done in the way of investigating that, other than continuing the psychoanalytic discipline and hoping that one would have some idea as to what the mind of a character is, or whatever it is to which we attach that name.

Audience member:

You speak of, or question, what language we are to use in interpretation, and you bring up the question of choice. How are we to choose? Now, you know, when courses are taught in technique, or supervision is given to candidates, or people are analysed, certain languages are used, and I would say that over the course of one's education one builds up an inventory of languages. If I were to consider the way that we talk to ourselves and our patients, our colleagues, our students, and so on, there may be thirty languages I use, and it is, in fact, an interesting exercise—maybe some of you have tried it—to codify those languages. In fact, you can recognise different analysts by the type of language they prefer to use. There are affect languages; they use a lot of affect in what they communicate. Then there are very cool intellectual analysts who use a certain style of analysing. Then there are, I would say, analysts who speak from a certain cluster of ideas, whose language arises from and touches upon that cluster of ideas in many different ways. I myself have been interested in listening to people in discussions and meetings, and I have made a list. I've counted about thirty different types of languages, some of which can be transformed into the others. I myself am not always sure. I'm not flexible enough to use more than five or six of these languages, and I'm not always sure which language to use when I think to myself or address somebody else. Sometimes it's a kind of reflex thing, and I don't think about it. But I wonder, would it help if there were an inventory of languages, if we put our heads together, would we arrive at not only thirty languages, but maybe fifty languages. That's where we have a problem. If we have to choose, it would be better if we knew what the mathematicians call the universe of discourse; if we knew what different languages there were that we might utilise and might find effective or helpful. So I would like you to consider whether there should be an inventory of languages, and whether, in fact, one does find oneself doing that intuitively, searching among one's own inventory of languages. That's the second question I wanted to ask.

The third question is: you said, Dr Bion, that we wait for patterns. Indeed we do. The problem develops—and I relate this to what I said about languages—if there are patterns that we already know about—we have a library of them in our heads—there's an oedipal pattern, let's say, and you see what happens. Some verbalisations and movements and affect is expressed and you say, "Ah-Ha! The oedipal pattern." So we wind ourselves up and we make the oedipal pitch. We have a library of patterns we have learned, and then there are a library of patterns we have grown up with, and there are a library of patterns that we find are characteristic of our thinking.

Now, considering that there are patterns and that they can be assembled into a library, the second part of it is that since each person we deal with is unique, as Dr Bion has emphasised, it is very likely that he or she is producing a pattern that we haven't thought of or experienced, and hence we cannot recognise, and all we can do after a while is recognise, not patterns, but repetitions. And are repetitions and patterns the same things?

Dr Bion responds:

It seems to me that the idea behind the psychoanalytic movement is that if one could go through having an analysis, one would get that much nearer to being sensitive to or susceptible to events, even mental events, which are occurring. Just like the clinician who is supposed to be trained to use his senses and to keep those senses in good working order. As a matter of fact, he isn't—trained in this way, I mean. Most of his time is spent being filled with a whole lot of stuff about medicine, so that there's no room for anything else. But, in fact, here and there people escape that and manage to preserve enough sensitivity to develop it further.

I'm sorry to sound so pessimistic about training and teaching, but I am much more convinced about one's ability to teach bad habits than I am of our knowledge or capacity to pass on something good. I think—and this seems to be the point about analysis—that one can remove oneself sufficiently to give the patient a chance, so that one's own obtrusive characteristics cease to interfere with the patient's possibility of developing themselves. I sometimes think of it in this kind of way. If you look, for example, at an unfinished piece of sculpture by Michelangelo, you can, in one instance at any rate, see that out of a bit of stone with all sorts of holes punctured in it, there are some human features emerging. Now it seems to me that a person like Michelangelo appears as if he were able to see those figures in the stone before he had done a thing to it, and what he does do is to enable the figures that are there to emerge, so that even people like myself can see them.

Now, this seems to me to be the kind of model which is possible within analysis. Can one have some sort of idea of the person that is hidden in this so-called neurotic chunk or this mass of psychosis? And if so, is there any way in which one could enable the real person to emerge out of that mass of stuff? That includes, of course, what he's been taught, what he thinks he's learned, or she thinks she's learned, in the course of his or her life. They very often have been taught or have learned things that are extremely wide of the mark, and they think they know themselves, but in fact we very often think it's more likely to be something else that they've got mixed up with. But they *don't* know who they are, and they may not be at all keen on finding out because of what happened to them last time, as it were. Of what happened in the words of this quotation here, you see: "In the mother's womb, man knows the universe and forgets it at birth." In the womb, man knows the universe. After birth, he's stuffed up with a whole lot of stuff that makes it impossible to see the universe at all. Not even the universe which is himself and of which he is the centre. He might as well be the centre of a galactic universe for all that he can see, simply because it is so crowded out there with what he has learned or thinks he's learned or has been taught.

Audience member:

Some of these far-out ideas begin to catch you after a while and are very engaging. I have the feeling that you were talking in some way about Michelangelo's *Prisoners*, as they were being released in statues, and suddenly some things began to make some sense so me. But they also stimulate other questions. And, as has been said, you're a trouble-maker. It seems to me that what we're talking about here is that the analyst begins to get a model of the human being's potentiality for growth, the so-to-speak, outer limits. He doesn't know if that will ever happen, but he can see the possibility. And at the same time you seem to have been speaking about a lot of existential moments, like a series of little growths, which can occur during the course of a successful analysis, or during the course of analysis. And so, in a sense, it's a lot of little happenings and it's not clear where they'll go, but in another sense it seems to be the potentiality for a model which is not a concrete model but sort of an outer limit model that the analyst has, if I refer it back to what you said. Michelangelo seems to know what he had in mind when he began his chipping away at his statue. I don't know if my question is very clear, but if my question isn't puzzled, I am.

Dr Bion responds:

Or he could dare to look at the block of marble—or whatever it is—until the pattern which was hidden in it emerges. If that is the case, then one could say there is something to be said for paying great attention for as long as one can to the person who comes for an analysis. For although one may not know, and in any case, one couldn't invent a person to take the place of whoever comes, at least one might in time be able to see what is there and always has been there, but for one reason or another has become hidden, even from the patient himself. One can say about the patient that the last thing they can do is to look into the centre of their souls or the centre of their minds.

In this collection of quotations here, there are some which are quite obviously derived from people with some kind of religious approach, whatever that is. But I think that you can see that there is a certain resemblance between these various approaches, particularly between those people who seem to be prejudiced, as it were, in favour of the truth. Rightly or wrongly there's an attempt to sculpt honestly, or to paint honestly, or to compose music with a certain degree of integrity. And in analysis, of course, one hopes that one at least tries to be honest. That's why I think that all this talk, which may have its proper place concerning analytic theories, is a waste of time. If you can *see* an interpretation, you ought to say it. You ought to express it. You ought to formulate it. If you don't see it, you're a fraud if you give the interpretation. In other words, whatever the interpretation is—Freudian, Abrahamian and so forth—you haven't got a right to give that interpretation unless you believe it is true. And if you don't believe it or can't see it, you've no right to give it. Because I think that one is under an obligation to be as truthful as possible—at any rate to refrain from deliberately making statements which haven't got, in our own opinion, backing from our own observation. But I think that I would put it to you that a really gifted person—a genius, really—*can* see in the bronze, or in the clay, or in the marble, or whatever it is, that which can't be seen by the rest of us until it is made manifest. Analytically, again, one hopes that one could reveal to the patient something which they haven't yet seen for themselves.

Audience member:

I'm struck by the similarity of some of the quotations with the mystical theology of the Catholic Church. To me, the language is reminiscent of people like St John of the Cross.

Dr Bion responds:

It's striking, that's true. It seems to me extraordinary that you get this with the mystics who are separated both in time and space in a most incredible way. If you read the description of Arjuna in the *Bhagavad Gita*, it's extraordinary how close the resemblance is, say, to Dante in his thirty-sixth stanza, or thereabouts, in the *Paradiso*. The same thing applies to Luria—Isaac Luria—who didn't even write anything down. All we know about him is what other people have reported about it. If you look at or read a thing like *Paradise Lost*, you can see Milton possibly struggling to conform to the Protestant religion. Gray could see quite easily that Milton was on the side of the devil all the time. He says so. That's another mystic. He's the person who is sensitive enough to understand Milton.

But it's extraordinary that people who are separated by so many hundreds of years express themselves in a recognisably similar manner, or so we think. One could say it's a matter of interpretation. But the whole point of reading people of that sort is that, again, one might just be able to detect something, some pattern that is repeated by other people as well. When I was at Oxford, I remember one of the dons there, to whom I was complaining that there wasn't time to read all the stuff that was to be read, replied, "You're quite right. There's no time for anything except the really *big* books." No good reading short ones; no good reading short analyses. Indeed, I think one thing we can teach people here is that time is of the essence. And you are probably familiar with this; if you are really tired, how much you slip into the habit of hunting around for some confounded interpretation or another to give, because you don't have the patience or you're too tired, and so forth, to listen in the hope that some interpretation will emerge. One really hunts around the library we keep in our minds instead of using our minds. We just use the stuff which is stored in it.

Audience member:

That's taking refuge in the interpretation instead of really letting it develop.

Dr Bion responds:

Well, I suppose it is. In other words, the interpretation can be just one more rationalisation. One more rational explanation. Because one lives in fear of the *irrational* and of things that do not oblige us by being comprehensible to the human mind. You want to go to read a book on astronomy and see that the universe and the stars are a lot of nonsense—the whole thing. But they happen to be a fact. We can dismiss the universe of a particular patient by saying it's a lot of nonsense; he's psychotic, finished. Full stop. Diagnosis achieved—sure—by the analyst. But what that particular patient is, is another matter.

Audience member:

What if one were fortunate enough to be able to discern a pattern that the patient is putting one in touch with—for example, that the patient speaks, and speaks in such a way that evokes visual imagery in the analyst. And later one is able to make the determination that the patient may have a particular purpose in eliciting visual imagery from the analyst, say, either to put the analyst to sleep, or something of that kind. Would it be possible to switch languages in the form of interpretation not just simply to call it to the attention of the patient, but to actually perform some sort of action by virtue of the interpretation, switching the language so that the nature of the space in the room has changed?

Dr Bion responds:

I suppose you could. For myself, you see, I feel that the best thing that I can do is to learn the English that I know as well as I possibly can. Unfortunately, that isn't very well. I was taught that it wasn't any good at any time, even in my school days. It's frightfully difficult to use a language anyhow which wasn't invented simply for the purpose of analysis. After all, a great deal of language has been invented for the purpose of lying, deception, evasion, trickery, and so forth. We ought, really, to be pretty good at all those things, but not good at speaking the truth. That, I think, is really going to be something which is difficult to get one's tongue around, because one is so unused to that. Or even hearing it. But this is a situation where we are really leading a sort of revolutionary attack, amongst other things, on the language itself and trying to turn it into a tool which is suitable for expressing the truth—if, of course, we knew the truth. It *is* such an important activity that we seem to have to learn to speak or to think before we can elucidate the truth. I've said it before, and I really don't know which comes first, but certainly it's a difficult business to find some method of communication even when one is trying to communicate with oneself.

So, while I can quite see that it might be better if I could play the piano, or if I could draw or paint, I find that I've got my work cut out even if I try to use such capacity to draw as I've already got properly. Meaning by that, the correct words at the correct time that I say properly. But I certainly wouldn't deprecate the idea of anybody who's gifted in that way developing those gifts and daring to use whatever gifts they've got.

Of course, the trouble is that so much of this is slanted because it is mixed up with learning to be an analyst, or something of that sort, but that is really slanting the whole thing. And we're allowed to pass it off and slant, as it were, the analysis in a way which may be of some use if the patient were going to *become* an analyst, but one doesn't even know very often whether the patient *ought* to become an analyst. Very often, they ought to become something quite different. Of course, when it comes to candidates, they've already been slanted, or slanted themselves—one doesn't know. But I don't see why an analysis shouldn't be an experience in which the patient discovers that their gifts lie in some other direction, whatever they're doing. When it comes to the individual analysis, even the individual who hasn't any doubt at all that he wants to be an analyst, it still isn't clear what sort of analyst he is to be. I should certainly dislike it very much if I felt that I wanted people to become analysts like me. I think it would be much better if they could become an analyst—if that's what they want to be—of a kind that would suit them and be really in accordance with their nature, like the piece of statuary that is in accordance with the block of marble out of which it is carved. I think I have said enough, and we will end the discussion here.

CHAPTER 3

Some problems of observation in treatment*

Wilfred Bion

The first thing I would like to say is that I think that I must be almost the only one participating in this series of lectures who is not a Kleinian. That may seem a bit odd when I go on and tell you that, in fact, I went to Mrs Klein for analysis. But Mrs Klein did not like being labelled a Kleinian. She strongly objected to it, and she said that she was just a psychoanalyst. However, not knowing very much about it, it did seem to me more and more as I had this experience of analysis with her, that I got the idea of what she was talking about when she said she was a psychoanalyst. Although the term itself is virtually meaningless, it's very convenient for talking *about* psychoanalysis. But what psychoanalysis itself is as an experience is another matter. There are plenty of people nowadays, however, who are Kleinians and who have had a Kleinian analysis and who *are* able to say something about that experience and what it feels like. What I want to do is to discuss for this short time that we've got here this matter of observation.

---

* This is a transcription of a lecture—the ninth in a series entitled *Kleinian Exploration in Human Intimacy*—delivered by Wilfred Bion at the Los Angeles Psychoanalytic Society and Institute (LAPSI) in 1975.

Now, there's no mystery about this. Scientists have always attached a great deal of importance to observation. Physically, this is fairly comprehensible. If somebody says they've got pain, you can say, "Well, where does it hurt?" and then you can go on from there. You can palpate them and look at them through a fiberscope, take the blood pressure, and so forth. I needn't bother you with all that because I think you're quite familiar with it.

One really wants to talk about observation, or when Freud speaks of psychoanalysis, of the scientific approach. He talks, or course, with great admiration of Charcot and Charcot's statement about *going on watching* until what is obscure begins to show itself as a pattern. I think that that itself gives a clue to the fact that Freud did indeed observe the human mind. The problem though is, what did it look like? And, you see, straight off I'm in difficulty because I talk about what it looks like, and these words are borrowed from the ordinary language in which one's talking about the physical appearance of something. What is the physical appearance of the mind? Well, supposing you watch a dog, the dog behaves in a peculiar way, and after a time I think that you'll begin to feel it's fair to say that the dog thinks or has a mind. Anyway, on that somewhat insecure foundation, you'll have to erect a scientific structure. I think it is very difficult to know what reply to make if somebody challenges you to say, "On what grounds do you call your observations the scientific observations of a mind?"

Now, at this point, I have to fall back on how things appear to me. Whether it'll be of any use to you or not, I don't know. But at any rate, what I'm trying to consider now is the order in which events appear to me. Of course, some of it is fairly simple. I'd say that one can see a patient who comes to see one; one can observe physical features and so forth. So you can give a verbal description of what you see. But as you do not know the patient or the analysand, or the person who comes to you for help, you're up against this problem of, *what is this*? What is this person who has come to see you or comes to seek your aid or help? To some extent, one can simplify this by saying that one is a psychoanalyst and one is concerned with the mind or character or personality of the person. But what does the character or personality of a person look like?

Borrowing from a sort of hint from what I understand of Kant, I would say that the first thing is an imaginative conjecture; that you imagine who or what this personality is. I think that if you continue to watch or observe as best you can, you might reach what I would call a rational conjecture, which I think makes a slight difference in what I'm talking about. But I don't think that conjectures of that nature would be accepted as being evidence of anything. You're in a very vulnerable position when you are wondering who or what this is that has come to see you if you have to fall back on imaginative conjectures, or even rational conjectures, if you think they're rational.

The situation gets more complicated when the analysand says that he had a dream. I can make further conjectures about what he means by that, but I also have doubts about his statement because it usually turns out that he means he fell asleep and he had a dream. I don't know on what grounds he categorises it as a dream or what validity to attach to a story about these events which, I gather, took place the previous night or whenever it was, whenever he *says* it was, but when he was in an entirely different state of mind. This story that I'm told, that he had a dream, is when he's wide awake. Now, this is typical and seems to me to be a description of a mental baby. Goodness knows what it's all about. I don't. But I can see that it's possible that when he is awake, there is some sort of debris left over of the experience of whatever it was when he was asleep.

Now, again, one has to look at these remnants, these vestiges, these leftovers from a quite different state of mind, because supported by Freud's original ideas, dreams are worthy of attention. I don't think you can deal with that by saying simply, "Oh well, you dreamt it. Period. Finished." Obviously, one's got to go further than that if, as seems to be the case, there's some validity in this idea that there are vestiges of something important, something valuable in this material. So as the patient goes on telling you that he had a dream, or that he had a most unpleasant experience, or that he's just seen some unpleasant accident in the road, I think one needs to sift it. One needs to have to look at it in order to preserve those elements in it which might be of value. I don't know quite why one should think that they might be of value excepting the fact that dreams seem to have excited the curiosity of human beings for a relatively long time. Freud seems to stress the importance of looking at dreams and interpreting them. That also has got a long history. After all, even in Genesis you get accounts of demands for the interpretation of dreams. One could also say that the curiosity about the dream, so-called, seems to be pretty well established in us. Sometimes you get a person who behaves in a way which I could call a dream, if only he were asleep. But he isn't. So one of the conditions which I think is necessary before one can say that one is dreaming isn't there.

And again, names are attached to these things like delusions, hallucinations, and so forth. It is supposed that a psychiatrist can take a scientific view and come to conclusions about whether the patient is hallucinated or deluded. Well, what's the difference between being deluded and simply being mistaken? I don't know, but what I want to draw your attention to here is the question, because perhaps somebody could make an approach towards helping us to know how to discriminate.

Anyway, to save time, we will just fall back on the languages that exist and on terms like delusions, dreams, hallucinations, and so forth, making any use that we can of the existing languages. Even psychoanalytic language. Psychoanalytic terms, like paramnesia and so on. I think Freud describes the paramnesia as something you can use to fill in a space which is a blank because you can't remember. It takes the place of the missing idea. But now again, I say, how do you tell the difference between the vast structure of the theories of psychoanalysis and a paramnesia. It certainly fills a space. It certainly fills a *mental* space. And nowadays we are able to talk using these theoretical terms, so one can go on elaborating this structure. I think Freud described it as … no, I think that Kant described it as an architectonic, a structure of the human mind. I think it would be very convenient indeed if one could have some idea of what that structure is. It's obviously a great advantage that very well illustrated books of anatomy exist. These pictures enable you to have an idea about things which seem not to fit in with that structure. If we knew what a mind was, then we could say, as you hear it working, betraying itself by talk and behaviour, and so on, in front of you, there's something a bit odd about what I can observe here, something which seems to depart from the mind as I understand it.

To come back to the practice of analysis as I understand it, listening to what I am told and going on the basis of the conversational behaviour which I can observe seems to me to betray something. There's something about the behaviour which may be very difficult to describe, and yet you can feel that there's something odd about the behaviour. It doesn't fit in quite with what you expect of a human mind or personality. Now, I said that it's very difficult to describe. I'm talking, of course, about a verbal formulation of it. That depends a great deal on the fact that even when I'm speaking what I consider to be the language that I know best, I don't find it easy to do at all. It becomes worse still if I would like to talk to somebody else about it, like talking to you about it here.

One of the clues that I collect or have collected is associated with what for want of a better word I would have to call beauty. I might be able to convey what I want to convey to you, if I could do it in the kind of way that artists seem to be able to do things. Now if you're going to be limited to verbal communication, which is usually the case, how are you going to command the artistic ability to express yourself? See, Shakespeare seems to be able to write case histories which are still interesting to read, although it's got a bit more complicated now because you have to employ people like actors and actresses who know how to read Shakespeare—we call it *perform* Shakespeare—in such a way that it could come to us what it was that he was talking about. I don't think anybody's going to read *my* scientific papers. And I don't think there's the slightest chance that I'll ever write a scientific paper that has sufficient scientific merit to get more than a passing glance from anybody. But this problem belongs to all of us if we want to communicate what it is that we see or hear. And there's another difficulty. Because as well as having something to convey, something to which one wants to draw attention, you have to have somebody to listen to what you say. There's got to be somebody who hears it.

Now, the person who hears it can interpret what they hear. I won't bother you with the many diagnoses I've heard of my own character or personality. I'm quite familiar with being told that I'm just crazy or nuts and so forth, but so far I've escaped, as it were, being incarcerated in a mental hospital. Partly because I've been lucky enough to be involved in cultures in which that isn't done, but after all, we all know that in Soviet Russia, apparently it is. So that state of mind, whatever it is, certainly seems to exist and makes it dangerous therefore to be in this vulnerable position where all you can fall back on is imaginative or rational conjectures about what you see or hear. In that state of affairs, I don't think it's possible to say that you *know* something. I think that you might go so far as to say it's *probable*. And mathematicians have even tried to elaborate theories of probability. The trouble, of course, with that method of communication is that it takes a long training or experience to understand the art of mathematics. However, it's awkward if you feel that there really *is* such a thing as mathematics.

People have manipulated numbers in all kinds of ways. In fact, ancient Hebrew literature is full of examples of it—of the use of numbers in a way with which we are not familiar today. Similarly, an outstanding person like Euclid produces a geometry which seems to be pretty satisfactory for a few hundred years, but gradually it becomes clear that it's inadequate. It breaks down over matters like parallel lines. And then you have to wait in the hope that somebody like Descartes will turn up who breaks through with his Cartesian coordinates which make it possible to make further advances. Now this doesn't mean that that mathematics didn't exist. It did. But it was implicit before somebody came along who could make it *ex*plicit.

Our problem is how to make it possible for somebody to come along who *may* understand what it is that we are trying to say. It's curious that so much depends on a collection of people, that the individual contribution is so trifling and the individual is so short-lived—so ephemeral—that it's most unlikely that he can solve a problem, but only that he might take it on from where it had got to. All this has become recently much more pressing. When I say recently, I mean within the last two or three hundred years. Because it seems pretty clear that there is a mind, and that it has got something to do with thinking.

I think that the philosophers, so-called, have appreciated this point for a long time and have attempted to think clearly themselves and even to persuade others to do likewise. However, there are other discoveries as well, and one of them could be said to be the discovery and practice of violence. Now the use of violence can be to provoke and evoke very powerful feelings, and it is very difficult indeed to think clearly when your powerful emotions have been stirred up. In extreme positions, I think everybody's familiar with it. You don't really think clearly when you're in fear for your life. So, from this point of view, there seems to be a tremendous advantage in being able to be a terrorist. You can put a stop to people who want to think or debate or discuss by simply arousing sufficiently powerful feelings of fear to overwhelm the capacity for thinking clearly.

Militarily, this kind of thing is dealt with by what we call discipline. People are drilled and drilled and drilled so that they have a kind of automatic response which enables them to tolerate or be unaware of the dangerous situation. But what's to happen then with this imaginative conjecture? Because that seems to me to lay the gate wide open for absolutely undisciplined thinking. And this is what I think that any really practised scientist would be up against in the attempt of a psychoanalyst and psychoanalysis to be scientific. I think that you do have to have some capacity for withstanding that pressure. And it isn't, I think, peculiar simply to psychoanalysis.

I remember a play of Emlyn Williams, more or less autobiographical really, in which a Welsh miner is seduced by a young woman. The actress who played the part of the seducer was very highly technically qualified, very capable. I say *technically* qualified. Now in London, that posed no particular difficulty. But when this play was transferred to Wales, and the hero was a Welsh boy who was being seduced, the feelings that were stirred up there by that presentation were quite unmistakable, so much so that the protection which is afforded by being on the stage seemed to be somewhat flimsy. However, that particular actress was, I think, a real actress and did not depart at all from the hideous character she was portraying. When that part was played, as it had to be once or twice by an understudy, the understudy was also a very capable actress, very technically equipped. But when the audience rose against her, she flinched. That seems to me to illustrate the difference between technical equipment and something else. I don't know how one would describe this something else, but it is absolutely unmistakable.

When I knew, in the sense of the sort of close contact that you have when you're being analysed by Melanie Klein, it seemed to me that she did not flinch. She gave very provocative and evocative interpretations. I can't say I liked them much myself but I grew to admire, after I had finished my analysis, the way in which she stood up to it. I wonder whether Strachey didn't describe something of the same kind when he talks about Freud's discussions with Stekel and Jung when they decided that Freud was entitled to use the term psychoanalysis—that he was the person who was most entitled to use it. Because Strachey describes a situation in which he thinks that Freud began to show signs of the constancy of these attacks. I think that by that time Freud was already even physically ill. But one can see that it can be very difficult to withstand that sort of attack. These *continued* attacks.

I'd like to put the problem perhaps more simply by taking up something more extreme. What are you to do if, as people engaged in this kind of work, one wants to stick to discussion within the limits of fairly ordinary civilised behaviour—ordinary politeness and so on. It seems hard to believe that the attempt to behave in a civilised manner is going to stand up against barbarism. I've had a little dose of this kind of thing, in which it is very *very* difficult to go on thinking clearly in a situation in which you feel that the next moment will probably be your last. I don't know how serious the situation is today with regard to this attempt to discuss these mental difficulties, really the *suffering* of the person. As likely as not, even your patient is liable to make you forget that in fact you're dealing with a suffering person who wants help. So while in theory one can go on giving one's interpretations, in practice, I'm not so sure. Certainly not in *my* practice, anyway. Because I find that the emotional situation is a very powerful one. It's misleading because, you know, in an office one is usually pretty comfortable, circumstances are quite simple, and there's nothing particularly alarming or unpleasant about it. But if you are sensitive to these peculiar things—I don't know what you call them—these mental phenomena, then you can feel the pressure on you all the time to depart from the limitations of civilised or polite behaviour. In other words, putting it in rather extreme language, the civilised person is under pressure to become uncivilised.

Now, in my mind, I am struck by a rather curious reminiscence of the remains, or the vestiges of biochemistry, which I'm supposed to have learned, about adrenalin and the adrenals and so forth. But what has that got to do with the mind, anyway? You can narrow down the view that one is only concerned with the mind. Not this stuff—biochemistry and the rest of it—that can be all right as a kind of theoretical mental construct that is quite convenient for putting things into packets in the kind of way one does when one talks about fear or sex or love or hate. But in reality, it isn't like that at all. In reality, although it may be just an ordinary conversation that you're having, your adrenals may be working overtime, and you can have pretty considerable pressure working from within. Either to fight the person or the state of affairs that you find yourself in, or to run away from it.

I think that if you're a practising analyst, especially in your more vulnerable and inexperienced years, you can feel that the pressure on you is sufficiently great to make you want to leave the room. Fortunately, of course, there's a plentiful supply of rational explanations of that. You can say you want to go to the loo, and so forth. You can produce quite convincingly, you hope, statements to explain your departure from the room. Unfortunately, since one is dealing with a human being, and as I think there is very little evidence indeed to suggest that the sort of people who come to us for help are stupid, it is very unlikely that they would be deceived by that subterfuge. And it isn't at all good for them anyway if they are able to be deceived by that subterfuge. Because theoretically, as I understand it, we are supposed to be truthful. So these lies and deceptions and subterfuges and so forth are not really available to the person who aspires to be helpful—the doctor or psychoanalyst.

One wonders what it is that makes an analyst an analyst—a *good* analyst. What makes an actress a good actress? Certainly not a technical ability. It happens to be quite a serious matter because, you know, the language of psychoanalysis can be very easily acquired, technically. I remember the times when one heard these phrases that, even then, had a rather hollow sound, like *father figure* and so on and so forth, which became almost part of the jargon of the time. And that kind of thing is what contributes to psychoanalysis being very rapidly in danger of extinction. Extinction by the mere fact of it being so easy to appear to be a good analyst by virtue of having all the clichés at your disposal.

Can one be dependent on some kind of a series of happy accidents, or is there any way that one could cultivate or foster the qualities that could lead to somebody being a *real* analyst or a *real* mathematician or a *real* painter or a *real* musician and not simply an artificial representation of an analyst or an artificial representation of an actor? The difficulty is that these artificial representations can easily be introduced into the culture itself. And there it seems to me that you're up against a problem—that is, whether the individuals or a certain sufficiency of individuals in the culture, or those who make up the community, have a capacity for discrimination and are able to detect the artificial representation of whoever or whatever it is, as well as the real thing.

Of course, with oneself, you can try to cultivate a capacity which would enable you to know when you're just being bogus or when you're really on the right track. I don't know what that is, but I don't think it is adequately discussed. Perhaps there's somebody here who would tell me if it's correct to say that the term *arbitean* refers to what is thought to be a part of the human mind which distinguishes. But, curiously, it doesn't seem to me to be quite the thinking, but closer to a feeling: that you *feel* that you're on the right track, or you *feel* that you're on the wrong track. I think the Chinese described it as *Tao*. In the *Tao Te Ching* there's quite a lengthy description which is more, I think, poetical than scientific, as we would understand it, but which is an attempt to formulate the existence of something that is *the way*. This crops up in all kinds of places, in all kinds of cultures. There seems to be a recognition of something that is *the right way*.

Now, as far as the individual is concerned, what would enable him to know when he is on that track, when he is on that *way*, and when he has diverged from it? I think that probably each individual has to consider his own experience in this respect. And how much can he rely upon whatever it is that enables him to feel that he's on the right track or off of it? Well, that involves being aware of yourself. And for some reason, it does seem as if the awareness needs to be formulated by such means at your disposal; musical composition, mathematical composition, painting, or verbal formulation. So of course, when it comes to verbal formulations, we're having to fall back on a relatively recently acquired capacity. I don't know what sort of dates could be ascribed to the capacity for thinking and also for verbal formulation, but certainly it's quite a recent acquisition. There again is a further problem. According to Mendel, certain characteristics are transmittable by generation. It used, at one time, to be thought that this didn't apply to acquired characteristics, but I'm not so sure about that. It seems to me that acquired characteristics *are* transmittable.

Moderator:

I think we will take a ten-minute break and then try to accommodate as many questions as possible.

Audience member:

Did I understand you to say that the patient knows when he has the right helper? How about people who continually connect with the wrong helpers, who seem to repeat the experience the patient originally had with a parent who was not a good enough mother or was thought to be so? These people stick to the bad parent/therapist and can't connect with the healthy nourishing one. I would appreciate a comment.

Dr Bion responds:

It would seem to me there are two or three points which are involved with this. One of them depends on the patient—who the patient *is*. That, as you can see, is a difficult business. It requires an entire analysis to get anywhere near who the patient is. But the point is when there are enough points of evidence that would lead you to feel the direction in which the patient was travelling. Now, when the patient gives you an indication that they are liable to choose the wrong person, one question that arises is, what is the driving force behind that. The other point could be that you can see that the patient doesn't really mean to choose the wrong person. They just aren't good at choosing the right one.

Here I would like to draw attention to one of the difficulties, it seems to me, that crop up in thinking about this kind of thing. We speak of a patient as *idealising* somebody. Yes, but there must be something behind that if the patient is idealising somebody. Something like a realisation that there is something *better than* real people. And the need for having a contact with something better than real people can make the patient idealise the analyst. Can make him make the best of a bad job although he feels that the analyst is like anybody else or worse— nonetheless, his craving to believe in something good would lead him to persist in the belief that the analyst and psychoanalysis are something good. You have to make allowances for that peculiar slant. And indeed, one of the points is really the analyst's need to get what I call a vertex—a point of view—from which you can see something which you can't see from a more ordinary vertex or position of seeing. It requires a certain degree of affectability or mental mobility by which you can change from a position where you can't see anything to another one where it gets clearer.

Moderator:

Dr Grotstein, you would also like to say something about this question?

Dr Grotstein:

No, not about this.

Moderator:

All right, do you have another question then?

Dr Grotstein:

Yes. My question is about how to account for the transmission of acquired characteristics genetically, one of the last things Dr Bion referred to in his discussion.

Dr Bion responds:

The question is, can one answer that problem within the frame of reference of how you can explain it genetically? I don't know that it can be explained genetically because the theory that I'm more familiar with is the Mendelian theory which seems to be varied over quite a large area of phenomena, but not on this one. In fact, I think there's got to be a change of ideas about what is transmissible because the theory of Mendelian inheritance isn't wide enough. I don't think it's adequate to explain. In much the same sort of way as you could do in geometry, it turns out not to be in a position to explain certain phenomena which are apparent, as to do with parallel lines. So I think that either one has to know a great deal more about the nature of genetic inheritance, or one has to revise one's views of what constitutes genetic inheritance or genetic transmission. I think we will end here.

CHAPTER 4

Notes on the diagnosis and psychoanalytic treatment of borderline patients: The Franz Alexander Memorial Lecture in Los Angeles*

Herbert Rosenfeld

I am glad to be able to speak to you today and so honour the memory of Franz Alexander. I had prepared a clinical theme, but only a fortnight ago I was asked to give you a scientific and theoretical paper on the psychoanalytic treatment of borderline and psychotic patients which would have taken many months to prepare. This paper is an attempt to fulfil your requirements and so remains a compromise; I shall tell you some of my diagnostic observations, experiences, and difficulties in the psychoanalytic treatment of borderline psychotic states. I shall also deal with the psychoanalytic view of narcissistic states with particular emphasis on their differential diagnoses.

The literature on this subject has grown to gigantic proportions, ever since Hughes in 1884 spoke of the "borderland of insanity". The first analytic attempt to define more clearly the group of patients who did not fit either into psychoneurotic or psychotic groups was made by Stern in 1938 in his paper "Psychoanalytic Investigation of and Therapy

---

* This lecture was delivered by Herbert Rosenfeld at the Los Angeles Psychoanalytic Society and Institute (LAPSI) in 1976. A version of the lecture was subsequently printed in 1977 in *The Bulletin of the British Psychoanalytical Society*.

in the Borderline Group of Neuroses". He discussed here a group of patients who were resistant to psychoanalytic treatment. He described them as being highly narcissistic, greatly oversensitive, and suffering from psychic "bleeding". They were paralysed by psychic trauma, rigid in mind and body, deeply insecure, masochistic, and suffering from deep-rooted feelings of inferiority. Stern was particularly impressed by the strength of the negative therapeutic reactions which predominated in these patients. It predominated over their capacity to make adequate use of the treatment situation. He also observed the tendency of such patients to use projective mechanisms, and he stressed their difficulties in reality testing, particularly in personal relationships. He obviously regarded the problem of narcissism as a major factor, but one is impressed by the similarity of his patients with Freud's rigid and inert group of patients who also showed marked negative therapeutic reactions. Freud's findings were described in the paper "Analysis Terminable and Interminable". Freud did not connect this deep resistance to narcissism, but rather to "the power in mental life" which he called "the instinct of aggression or of destruction".

In my papers on narcissism (1964), on the negative therapeutic reaction (1968), and on examining the aggressive aspects of narcissism (1971), I investigated in some detail severe chronic obstacles to treatment including the negative therapeutic reaction created by narcissistic structures. I found that a detailed psychoanalytic investigation of a number of patients who presented chronic resistances to analysis by acting out and by narcissistic withdrawal states, helped me to discover narcissistic structures which I linked with Freud's observations about the clinical importance of the instinct of destruction and his contention that most phenomena of life could be explained by the concurrent and/or mutual opposing action of two primary instincts. It would be exaggerated to claim that all severe narcissistic patients respond to analytic treatment.

Kernberg describes narcissistic patients functioning at an overt borderline level who show chronic narcissistic rage which is often expressed quite openly and where antisocial and sadistic sexual behaviour combined with violence may be prominent. He feels that these cases usually present a contraindication for analysis, often even for the modified psychoanalytic procedure which he recommends for most borderline patients. I agree with Kernberg that violently aggressive patients, particularly those who act out with physical violence with the analyst, are generally unsuitable for analysis, particularly if they deliberately try to wreck the treatment situation. Some violent patients, however, occasionally respond to analysis if the parameter is introduced that treatment could be discontinued unless the physically destructive behaviour can be controlled. There are also certain severely sadistic and masochistic patients who do not respond to analysis.

I have had the opportunity to observe the treatment of at least one severely destructive narcissistic patient who preferred to continue to adhere to the idealisation of his omnipotent destructive and self-destructive powers, and who after some improvement, refused all analytic and psychotherapeutic help, gave up his achievements in life including his close relationships, and drifted away into a rigid, aggressive inertia which was accompanied by a constant preoccupation and idealisation of death which, after some delay, actually ended in death. This patient could be called a case of extreme destructive narcissism; and such an outcome of analytic, psychotherapeutic, and psychiatric treatment of narcissistic patients is rare. Even an obstinately destructive attitude often softens, and life is allowed to return. Generally, I have found that narcissistic patients improve considerably during analytic treatment.

During the last ten to fifteen years there have been many reports of successful analytic treatment of narcissistic patients particularly by Kernberg and Kohut who have differentiated the narcissistic character disorders from the borderline group of patients. These analysts feel that analytic treatment is now the treatment of choice of narcissistic patients. Kernberg's theory of narcissism is closely related to my earlier work on narcissism of 1964. Both Kernberg and I myself have tried to clarify pathological narcissism, but there is still a great deal of work to be done. I have studied Kohut's work in some detail and believe that many of the narcissistic self-structures, such as the grandiose self, which he regards as normal archaic parts of the self, are in fact pathological narcissistic structures. I agree with Kohut that it is extremely important to diagnose narcissistic rage and differentiate it from other sources of hate or anger. What I have found missing in his work is the description of the working through in analysis of narcissistic rage and the negative transference that is related to this problem. Kohut discusses destructive omnipotent narcissistic structures and personalities in relationship to dictators and organisations such as Hitler and Nazi Germany, but he has not applied his views to clinical pathology.

The understanding of destructive narcissistic structures plays a central part in the treatment of psychosis, but it is also essential for the analysis of many chronic neurotic conditions, perversions, drug addictions, and certain borderline states. I shall now turn to observations on the diagnosis of borderline states. I think it is important for us to realise that there are many different types or groups of borderline states, and many analysts use the term borderline for patients who show a number of psychotic features without being overtly schizophrenic or psychotic. I sympathise and agree with Robert Knight who said in 1953 that "The term borderline case is not recommended as a diagnostic term and a much more precise diagnosis should be made which identifies the type and degree of psychotic pathology." His paper illustrates the difficulties of a highly experienced psychiatrist and therapist in arriving at the differential diagnosis of latent psychosis, particularly of schizophrenia, early schizophrenia, mixed neurotic and psychotic states, and borderline conditions. In the diagnosis of borderline states he stresses the importance of a number of impaired ego functions such as lack of achievement over long periods of time, combined with vagueness and unreality of plans for the future and insufficient contrast between dream content and waking activities. He also describes the presence of multiple symptoms and disabilities, especially if these are too easily accepted as ego syntonic by the patient or, on the contrary, viewed as being due to "malevolent external influences".

In contrast to many other psychiatrists and analysts, Frosch in 1964 and Kernberg in 1967 and 1968 described specific character structures to clarify the diagnosis of the borderline patient. Frosch suggested that the term psychotic character be substituted for that of borderline state as well as ambulatory schizophrenia, pseudo neurotic schizophrenia, schizophrenia without psychosis, latent psychosis, larval psychosis, "as if" characters, and neurotic ego distortions. He thought the symptom or cluster of symptoms were not suitable for classification. He felt that there was a definite entity or syndrome characterised by ego functions in their relationship to reality, other objects, and other psychic structures.

Under certain conditions patients may develop transient psychosis, but he found it equally possible for such an individual to go all his life without developing a psychosis. Frosch does not recommend psychoanalysis but psychoanalytic therapy for the psychotic character syndrome.

Kernberg similarly describes patients who have a rather specific stable pathological personality organisation, which he calls "borderline personality organisation". Kernberg's patients present with neurotic symptoms including anxiety, polymorphous perverse sexuality, schizoid or hypomanic pre-psychotic personalities, impulse neurosis and addiction, infantile and antisocial character disorders, and many polysymptomatic problems such as phobias, obsessions, dissociations, and paranoid trends. All these symptoms were occasionally present in varying combinations but did not help to differentiate the syndrome. He finds the borderline cases are easily differentiated from psychosis but not as easily from neurosis. He insists that borderline patients do not even under stress develop the self and object mergers which are typical for psychosis. He gives a very detailed picture of the ego and general character structure of the borderline patient. He stresses, for example, non-specific manifestations of ego weakness represented particularly by their lack of anxiety tolerance and lack of impulse control. He describes the predominance of early ego defences such as splitting of objects into good and bad, primitive idealisation, early forms of projection (in particular projective identification), denial, and omnipotence. Kernberg found that when analysis was attempted, these patients often developed a transference psychosis characterised by a particular loss of reality testing and even delusions restricted to the transference situation. He also emphasised that the borderline patient often develops a particular acting out of his instinctual conflicts in the analytic transference, which gratifies his pathological need and blocks further analytic progress. Kernberg finds psychoanalytic treatment contraindicated and recommends carefully directed psychoanalytically orientated psychotherapy. He suggests a detailed elaboration of the latent and manifest negative transference followed by the deflection of the manifest negative transference away from the therapeutic interaction by systematically examining it in the patient's relationship with others. I am impressed by both Frosch's and Kernberg's careful work. I do agree that in general symptoms are not the best guide for diagnosing the borderline patient.

I have, however, seen so many different types of borderline patients that I feel some classification is necessary and helpful to me and maybe also to others.

I suggest five groups of such patients. Contrary to Kernberg's experience, in my first group I would place patients whom I find very difficult to differentiate from the latent psychotic state. In the second group I would place most of the patients whom Kernberg and Stern describe. These patients usually have an infantile character and show generalised lability and oversensitivity. They show an infantile demandingness and overinvolvement and often an exhibitionistic dependency and clinging to objects. Sometimes a mixed depressive paranoid masochistic character structure predominates. Sometimes they suffer from what Stern calls "psychic bleeding". They feel wounded, and hurt, and their mental skin does not protect them against any slight injuries from the external world, but equally they cannot keep what they have been given. It constantly seems to leak out and so increases their demandingness. In the third group I place the "as if" patient who seems to be difficult to diagnose in a psychiatric interview so that he is frequently only really recognised during an analysis. Here I am in agreement with Grinker (Grinker et al., 1968) who has placed this type of patient into a separate grouping.

In the fourth group of borderline patients I would place those who suffered severe mental trauma in early infancy for long periods, sometimes for years. These patients have not only experienced insufficient mothering in early infancy but had to cope with long drawn-out separations in later childhood. They seem to have retained many of their early infantile psychotic mechanisms such as omniscient and omnipotent projective identification, used particularly to evacuate overwhelming anxieties into external objects and situations. These long separations from their mothers have prevented such patients from modifying their primitive modes of functioning with the help of external objects. On the contrary it seems that the later separation problems often increase the early psychotic anxieties and the primitive defence systems related to them. In addition, the normal oedipal problems are intensely reinforced, as absence of the parents makes it impossible to modify oedipal conflicts through the understanding help of the primary objects. In spite of the strength of their psychotic anxieties such patients feel that they have an inherent strength and reality sense because they have survived. They often have an intense narcissistic pride in having almost single-handedly kept themselves alive. This type of patient is very likely to develop some psychotic transference manifestations during analytic treatment, as the slightest positive change but also the slightest misunderstanding on the part of the analyst leads to violent primitive eruptions of the early psychotic anxieties.

In the fifth group I would place patients who show a mixture of narcissistic modes of functioning combined with the problems described by Kernberg, such as marked ego weakness, inability to sustain interest, and feelings of inner emptiness that lead to excessive dependency on external object relationships which, however, they find extremely difficult to maintain. It is a mixture of an intense need for objects, and an overpowering narcissistic withdrawal reaction, which dominates the life and treatment situations of these patients. This mixture of inertia and intense violent emotional reactions often has a psychotic intensity and leads to the patient being diagnosed as psychotic or schizophrenic, and in its turn to long hospitalisation. In my experience these patients are definitely borderline, but they do not develop a severe transference psychosis. It is their acting out which may be analytically difficult to control and which may require temporary hospitalisation. The five groups of borderline patients which I propose frequently overlap and may, therefore, cause some diagnostic confusion. They all have one important factor in common: they are difficult to treat. But it is interesting and gratifying that the detailed psychoanalytic treatment of these patients is not as impossible and hopeless therapeutically as Stern, and later Knight and Kernberg, seemed to believe.

Group one

I shall now turn to some clinical observations of the five different groups of patients that I have described. In my analytic and supervisory work I have been most familiar with borderline patients who have a psychotic character structure. They use psychotic mechanisms freely and often have beliefs which do not differ a great deal from psychotic delusions, but generally these delusional beliefs are projected into real-life situations where they can be hidden. This gives the patient a certain stability and pseudo sanity. Sometimes the delusion relates to a magical union frequently eroticised with an omnipotent idealised object. In my experience, once the split between a massively idealised object and the real object has been worked through, in particular in the transference, we are then faced with an upsurge of severe persecutory anxieties. There is, of course, always the danger that the real object represented by the analyst in the transference may now become the persecutor, particularly when the delusional union with the idealised object is gradually revealed in the treatment. If this appears at a time in the analysis when some trust in the helpful aspects of the analyst has evolved, it is not likely that a paranoid transference would develop, but one has to be on the lookout for the paranoid anxieties which will appear simultaneously with the revelation of the magically idealised delusional object. If the highly erotic delusional object relation attaches itself to the analyst there is a danger of a highly eroticised transference psychosis. This outcome does not generally occur in the borderline psychotic states, unless there has been a marked collusive relationship with the analyst previously. In the successful treatment of the psychotic borderline state, the revelation of the delusional object relation often increases confidence in the analyst as a real object and a more realistic therapeutic alliance can develop. Technically I think it is essential in borderline states of this kind to be firm, open, and perceptive to the intense fear and pain that patients have to go through when they become aware of the content of their delusional dream state. This makes them feel temporarily quite mad. It is also important to realise that these patients, even if they want to be helped by the analyst to return to life, temporarily experience a breakthrough to better understanding as a persecution, and this often leads to confusion and negative therapeutic reaction. The negative therapeutic reactions are generally related to the power of the delusional omnipotent dream state, which is opposed to reality and life, and any dependent relationship to the analyst generally stands for the feeding mother.

Group four

The traumatised patient of group four has many features in common with the psychotic borderline group. He is more in contact with the infantile nature of his feelings. All his emotions, his anxieties, pain, hate, and guilt have an overwhelming quality. He deals with emotions, in particular with the overwhelming anxieties, by violent omnipotent and omniscient projection into other objects or situations, in order to deny their existence and make their content unknown. Only then does he hope to feel better. This violent expulsive process of mental content creates emptiness and incapacity to think which he tries to overcome by omnipotently taking over (stealing) and copying the mind of an idealised object in a secret manner. This process creates intense guilt as the normal infantile self and the relationship he tries to form to a caring object is thus eliminated or destroyed. Analysis with these patients creates difficulties because interpretation of the denied and unknown mental content is contrary to the patient's insistence on denial and anonymity. This insistence causes intense anxiety and resentment because the patient feels the analyst should play the role which he, the patient, assigns to him—namely to allow the mental content to remain unknown. Consequently, the analyst's interpretative function can cause a great deal of confusion and misunderstanding. As the patient mainly functions through omnipotent processes, he believes that the analyst functions similarly. This belief is reinforced through the patient's projective processes so that the analyst's image becomes confused or fused with the omnipotent self of the patient. When this happens, a transference psychosis becomes manifest which has a paranoid character, where the analyst is constantly experienced as asserting that he is right in everything he says and that the patient is wrong. The analyst's behaviour, his speech, and his thoughts are constantly tested by the patient for proof that he has omnipotent characteristics himself, so that any interpretation of projection is suspected and counteracted and is then thrown back at the analyst who is accused of denial of his own omnipotent problems.

The danger of a lasting deadlock in the analysis can be avoided by giving the patient time to get over the confusion, by allowing him to express his anger, observations, and criticisms without attempting more than tentative infrequent interpretative work. This means that it is analytically essential to help the patient to bring his or her often completely distorted image of the analyst right into the open, which helps the patient to experience the analyst as a receptive and accepting person who can contain the patient's projection. A too-immediate interpretation of projection often has the opposite effect, namely the creation of a rejecting image of the analyst. One has also to remember that links between different parts of the self are being violently attacked during the delusional episode. This is one of the reasons for the patient's inability to use normal self-observation. They may have the conviction that good aspects of the self have been lost forever, but they may not observe that they themselves have been responsible for this attack. They feel persecuted by the analyst's overinterpretation of aggressive parts of their personality and believe him to be responsible for the attack on their good self. If it is possible to show the patient, often through a dream, that he or she believes that positive (particularly loving) infantile aspects of the self have been lost and killed by themselves forever, they may be able to acknowledge the correctness of the analyst's observation even if the conviction continues, but the interpretation may shake the patient's delusional conviction that the analyst is wanting to kill them with his interpretations.

My experience with some borderline patients particularly in groups one and four contradicts Kernberg's observation that in the borderline states there exists mainly confusion of early pathological part-object relations with the analyst as a result of splitting and projection of these objects. He states that such a situation in the transference may temporarily cause transference psychosis where the analyst "becomes" the bad object of the past, such as the mother. My own observations have shown that some splitting and projection of bad parts of the self occur frequently in borderline states, and confusion or merging of self and object may cause a transference psychosis which will probably only last a limited period when the cause of the confusion is carefully investigated by the analyst. Interpretations of the projective process as I previously explained are strictly contraindicated during the transference psychosis.

Group two

In relation to the second group of borderline patients which have a similarity to Kernberg's observations, I would like to stress that the patients' main difficulty appears to relate to containing their anxieties, dealing with separations, and their oversensitivity which causes any minor difficulty occurring in their lives to immediately appear to become a major catastrophe. Many patients in this group are so oversensitive that one feels they have hardly any mental skin, a problem which Stern has called "mental bleeding". This problem seems related to the patient's constant entanglement with situations or objects that show in reality a striking similarity to aspects of the patient's own personality, which the patient wants to hide and disown. As a result of this projective process the patient seems stuck and unable to feel any distance from these objects. They feel irritable, constantly obsessionally preoccupied with the person or situation. While they cannot detach themselves from the person concerned, specific aspects of the patient's character which relate to the situation become increased rather than diminished by this process. Analysis of this problem is very difficult, as the patient feels easily criticised and rejected because they regard this problem as an inherent part of their personality which is unchangeable. In the analysis, these patients often give the impression that being in analysis means being there to stay, and they react for a long time to any interpretation of this attitude with intense feelings of being rejected. They tend to idealise the analyst as someone into whom they can project all their problems and difficulties, and as they can use the analyst as an idealised receptacle they subtly undervalue him as someone from whom they can accept nourishment, which allows them to become stronger. Insofar as these patients use the analysis endlessly to repeat their problems rather than to learn from their experience, they act out in the way Kernberg describes.

Another important problem of these patients is their intense desire to be part of the analyst's life situation. The patient often admits and helps in the analysis of this problem but maintains in a hidden way that he believes that he is the analyst's favourite so that he will never have to part from him. This secret conviction is often missed as it appears as projection into another patient who arouses intense jealousy. Another problem of these patients which becomes apparent only after a long analysis is their deep conviction that they are incurable, crazy, or mad, and that they have deceived the analyst about their pseudo sanity. When this problem gradually is brought to light the patient is often convinced that the analyst had colluded with them to keep this problem out of the analysis, probably because of the analyst's own fear of being psychotic himself. In the treatment of the borderline patient the extent to which the analyst unconsciously colludes in making the treatment more difficult probably varies a great deal. I think it is important to recognise that the borderline patient chooses a particular form of projection which often has a double meaning and has the effect of making the analyst miss the main points, which in turn increases the patient's omnipotent delusion that he can control the analyst's mind. In the analytic treatment it is essential to expose all evidence of entanglements and collusion which have attached themselves to the transference. This seems the only way to break the vicious circle. I cannot understand how Kernberg's suggestion of avoidance of analysing these problems in the transference can really help the patient because unconsciously this contrived process must increase the patient's conviction of his own omnipotence. It is the proof of his capacity to make the analyst helpless. For the patient, this unconsciously means that the analyst is the carrier of the patient's own madness.

Group three

Now I want to make some comments about group three, the "as if" personality. Many borderline patients have some "as if" features in their behaviour. But if the "as if" features dominate the personality of the patient, the analysis becomes very difficult. One of my patients made great sacrifices for his analysis, but for a long time he found it extremely difficult to cooperate. He complained that he frequently felt that he was drowning, disappearing into nothing. Whenever I wanted to confront him with any problem that appeared in the analysis he did, in fact, emotionally disappear. One of this patient's difficulties was related to his doubt that any strong emotions that he experienced were real. "Do I really feel anything, or do I just want you to believe that I experience love, depression, or any other feelings?" I believe that the "as if" patient is intensely narcissistic, but he deceives himself about this. It is apparently the domination by an omnipotent self which controls the perceptive apparatus and recreates the deception in the self-presentation and also the deception in the object relationship. This process creates uncertainty in the patient and in the observer. These patients are difficult to treat because they are constantly misleading to themselves and to the analyst.

Group five

The patients of group five often present a mixture of narcissistic problems—endless repetition of negative therapeutic reactions combined with disguised psychotic anxiety or delusion. One patient of mine whom I think belongs to this group has been in psychotherapy and psychoanalytic treatment on and off for more than fifteen years. Whenever she improved and had a chance to relate more to life, she became acutely anxious and withdrew into a sleepy state where she felt forced to retire to bed and feed herself on tranquilisers, food, and drink. She turned on all the heating equipment that she could lay her hands on. In this state her anxiety subsided and she was comfortable, but she found it difficult to make any effort to return to life again. Consciously she regarded her withdrawal to bed as an attempt to regain a comfortable womb or eggshell while she supplied all the warmth and food herself. Gradually we became aware in the analysis of an entirely opposite experience to that which was observable in this withdrawn phase. It was then shown to be in imprisonment or domination by an extremely powerful and destructive narcissistic organisation which threatened the patient with death if she tried to return to life. Even when she was better, she was not able to experience herself as really belonging to herself. She gradually became more aware that she had a disguised paranoid attitude to the world and all people whom she experienced as making demands on her to which she had to submit in a placatory way. This seemed to be identical to her behaviour towards the ideal and persecutory withdrawal state in which helpless surrender or appeasement was the predominant feature. Obviously, it was the domination of internal and external persecutory anxieties, which were disguised, that had prevented her from forming good object relations which could be internalised and help her to get stronger and independent.

Conclusion

It is not possible for me to summarise this paper, but it may have become clear that it seems to be a characteristic of all borderline conditions that the psychotic anxieties are carefully hidden in external reality situations. There is a strong desire in all borderline patients to pull the analyst into some collusive relationship where he may act out with the patient without being aware of it. I therefore suggest that it is not only the projective elements in the analysis of borderline patients which make the analysis of the transference so difficult. Another essential aspect characteristic for all borderline conditions is the failure to internalise good objects which are necessary to strengthen the ego. This is not only due to the reaction of the narcissistic organisations who attack any meaningful dependent relationships to objects and the analyst, but to the excessive projection of hidden psychotic—particularly paranoid—aspects of the self into external objects in a hidden way which makes *any object dubious and uncertain*. This shows itself particularly during separations where the apparent good internalisation of the analyst quickly disappears and gives rise to intense but often unknown anxiety, which if more clearly examined reveals the hidden paranoid feelings of the patient that are so carefully disguised. I suggest that it is important to pay attention to the entanglements of the projection of the patient with certain real events or characteristics of the analyst or other objects which represent the analyst in the outside world. This has to be carefully observed and fully understood to help the patient to develop and to cope with life.

References

Freud, S. (1937c). Analysis terminable and interminable. *S. E., 23*: 209–254. London: Hogarth.

Frosch, J. (1964). The psychotic character. *Psychiatric Quarterly, 38*(1): 81–96.

Grinker, R. R. (1968). *The Borderline Syndrome. A Behavioural Study of Ego Functions*. London: Basic Books.

Grinker, R., Weble, B., & Drye, R. C. (1968). *Borderline Syndrome: A Behavioral Study of Ego-Functions*. New York: Basic Books.

Hughes, C. (1884). Borderline psychiatric records: prodromal symptoms of psychical impairment. *Alienist and Neurologist*, July: 85–91.

Kernberg, O. (1967). Borderline personality organization. *Journal of the American Psychoanalytic Association, 15*: 641–685.

Kernberg, O. (1968). The treatment of patients with borderline personality organization. *International Journal of Psycho-Analysis, 49*: 600–619.

Knight, R. P. (1953). Borderline states. *Bulletin of the Menninger Clinic, 17*(1): 1–12. Also in: R. M. Loewenstein (Ed.), *Drives, Affects, Behavior* (pp. 203–215). New York: International Universities Press.

Rosenfeld, H. (1964). On the psychopathology of narcissism: a clinical approach. *International Journal of Psychoanalysis, 45*: 332–337.

Rosenfeld, H. (1968). Notes on the negative therapeutic reaction. Paper read to the British Psychoanalytical Society and to the Menninger Clinic, Topeka, Kansas.

Rosenfeld, H. (1971). A clinical approach to the psychoanalytic theory of the life and death instincts: an investigation into the aggressive aspects of narcissism. *International Journal of Psychoanalysis, 52*: 169–178.

Stern, A. (1938). Psychoanalytic investigation of and therapy in the borderline group of neuroses. *Psychoanalytic Quarterly, 7*(4): 467–489.

CHAPTER 5

On autism*

Donald Meltzer

Last night I tried to develop for you particularly the theme of Mrs Klein's discoveries, as it were, of the spaces of the mind—the geography of phantasy—and to trace for you its implications for the concept of psychopathology and phenomenology related to these different spaces. Tonight I want to try to develop the next theme, which is really in a sense the discovery of spacelessness, that is also, I think, the discovery of mindlessness. And I want to try to show you how this was developed, because it developed with a certain degree of discreteness in two different people's work, although of course they were always in communication with one another a bit and influencing one another—fundamentally a really big influence by Dr Bion.

There was Dr Bion developing his theory of alpha function, the Grid, and the theory of container and contained, and there was Mrs Bick with her researches about skin containment, and myself with my group studying autistic children. And what came out of it was a very surprising

---

* This is a transcription of a lecture—the final lecture in a series of four—delivered by Donald Meltzer at the Los Angeles Psychoanalytic Society and Institute (LAPSI) on January 5, 1979.

convergence that seems to me to have opened up an annex, as it were, to the whole problem of the geography of phantasy that has brought psychoanalysis a bit more into a rapprochement with some of the problems being worked on in some of the centres of philosophical research these days having to do with linguistics and the ways in which language can be used and misused and the ways in which communication does and doesn't take place. This work brought into focus the concept of *meaning*. It seems to me that one can deal with Freud's model of the mind, as if it were a model that didn't necessarily deal with meaning in itself but really dealt fundamentally with impulse life and the gratification or frustration of impulse life, the generating of anxiety as a signal of danger, but the danger not necessarily being a danger that had any particular meaning in it. When you get to Mrs Klein's model, it really does change in a way that makes meaning the very centre of things. Emotionality becomes the most intense focus of the meaningfulness of what is going on in the mind.

Now in a sense, being brought up psychoanalytically in Mrs Klein's sphere and taking these spaces rather for granted, and in a sense therefore also taking the meaningfulness of mental life for granted, it did come as a very great surprise to me as I studied with my colleagues the phenomena thrown up in the treatment of this group of autistic children. And the whole process of the treatment of the children, the supervision of that treatment, and the seminaring of it took about ten years. It took about eight of those ten years for these things to begin to sink in—to myself and the rest of us—because it was such a departure from the habitual modes of thought and the general conception of mental life that we had prior to that. And that is, that we certainly did seem to discover the compelling evidence in the evolution of the treatment of these children and the phenomena of the transference as it evolved with them, that these were children in whom the absence of an internal space and therefore the absence of the capacity for projection and introjection seemed to be the main factor in the impeding of their developmental process. And that seemed to us to imply that either these children had regressed from what Mrs Klein had defined as the first step in developmental history—that is, the first splitting and idealisation and the first projections and introjections that accompany this splitting and idealisation—that it seemed to imply that either there was a regression from that position that caused a sort of collapse of the spaces inside the self and inside external objects, or that there was really a developmental step prior to splitting and idealisation that created these spaces into which projection and introjection could operate to create an internal world. By that time we understood very well that this internal world was really the place in the mind where the meaning of things was generated in unconscious phantasy which Dr Bion later described as Row C in his Grid, and that the first step beyond that was generated by alpha function.

It's true that in many of the histories of these children there did seem to be a history of an initial advance in their development and then some sort of collapse and regression. And I don't think we ever came to any absolute conviction within ourselves as to whether the spacelessness that we observed in these children was developmental, an impedance of a primary developmental step, or whether it was a regression from a position that was given by what Dr Bion would call a preconception, that a preconception of spaces would find its immediate realisation simply in the act of birth. I must say that seems most likely to me. But I don't think it matters essentially whether spacelessness is a primary developmental situation that then has to be expanded into spaces, or whether it's something that happens as a result of some sort of collapse of the spaces that have their origins in this first realisation of the process at birth. The thing that mattered to us really was the phenomena that we saw for the first time in these children that seemed related to spacelessness. That is, that we did think that we saw in these children an incapacity to function at a level that had meaningfulness as its focus and that in its place they function at a level that had either meaningless behaviour or imitative behaviour.

Now, this imitative behaviour, the mimicry, the things that we observed for instance in these children that were so striking was one of automatic imitation of things—like a child watching branches swinging in the wind and immediately swinging with them, or watching somebody sweeping the leaves outside the consulting room and immediately making sweeping motions and so on. We felt at that time that we were seeing something in the nature of mimicry that had to do with the perception of the external formal qualities of objects and their movement or behaviour, but that had nothing to do with the meaning of this behaviour.

At the same time, Mrs Bick was struggling to understand phenomena that she was seeing in certain of her patients, primarily a very schizophrenic girl that she had for years, but also surprisingly similar phenomena in much more ordinary neurotic patients, but neurotic patients of a particular sort—patients that seemed to have a peculiar and unexplainable tendency to collapse and then to recover and collapse and recover. What she described, as you probably know from reading her great paper, is that she discovered that these people had a defect in the experience of the self as being well contained by their skin and that they felt neither well held together by a skin that functioned as an exoskeleton, you might say, nor had they reached the stage of development where they were well held together by identification with internal objects as a kind of endoskeleton to their personality.

These people whom she did describe as having this leaky kind of skin were having repeated experiences of collapse, of leaking, of vomiting, incontinence of urine on the street, or a tendency for nose and eyes to run—all of those sorts of phenomena of incontinent orifices. She also discovered that these patients, like our autistic children, manifest a certain tendency for automatic types of identification. She named it adhesive identification. And we picked up that name from her to apply to the phenomena of mimicry that we saw in the autistic children. Adhesive identification seems to me to be very different from projective identification. I don't think that, as far as the psychoanalytic literature is concerned, we are the first ones to describe this phenomenology. I mean, I think that it was very accurately described in Helena Deutsch's paper on the as-if personality. I always thought that paper could be subsumed under the phenomenology of projective identification, but when Mrs Bick described adhesive identification I could see very clearly that I had been mistaken about it, that Helena Deutsch had described imitative social behaviour in people who changed their behaviour with great facility to match the social behaviour of whatever group or culture they happen to enter.

And one sees this quite strikingly, for instance, in patients. I've had patients who came to England during the war as adolescent children and who learnt English—but *English* English—just like that. Whereas generally you would think that an adolescent child would not be able to learn a new language and its accents without great difficulty. But not only did they learn English just like that, they also forgot their mother tongue and later in life had to recover it. Sometimes accents of their mother tongue began to creep into their English. But these were the instances—that kind of change from one language to another—not only of picking up the grammar and the syntax, but picking up the music of it and speaking, as it were, better English than the English. This is also a manifestation of the capacity of some people to operate on the basis of mimicry, and this mimicry seems to be produced, as Mrs Bick described it, by a phantasy of sticking to the surface.

From the point of view of the history of the development of psychoanalytic thought, it means that Freud was in great difficulty trying to distinguish between narcissistic identification and introjective identification. He couldn't find the means to describe the difference between them. Mrs Klein, then, through this description of spaces, was able to describe a narcissistic form of identification—projective identification. And Mrs Bick was describing a second, more primitive form of narcissistic identification which is called adhesive identification.

Now, the thing that relates to spacelessness and to the problem of meaning and meaninglessness and of mentality and mindlessness is that adhesive identification manifests a mimetic identification with the surface appearance and behaviour of other people or things or animals; it certainly plays a part in a sense of culture in general. And this is an identification with the appearance of things having nothing to do with the meaning, nothing to do with the mental states of the particular person, say, who is being identified with. It doesn't have to do with mental states at all. It has to do with social appearances, and it is a method of social adaptation which some people are very, very skilful at. Projective identification is essentially concerned with mental states. The very object, the very purpose that lies behind the projective identification has essentially to do with the perception that the object is in a different mental state than the self, and that that mental state is coveted in some way—one wishes to invade it, to participate in it, to take it over. It is the capture of the mentality of the object that is the very aim of projective identification. I think that's something that we didn't quite realise about projective identification until we were in a position to compare it to this more primitive form of narcissistic identification and the mindlessness that it involved.

We came to these conclusions, that these autistic children were having a great difficulty in expanding the flatness of themselves and their objects and creating a space, and then further, having difficulty in closing the orifices of themselves and their objects so as to create continent spaces that could contain something. It did make us realise for the first time that there was a problem of dimensionality that really needed to be examined and scrutinised in the whole realm of mental functioning and personality functioning—that we couldn't content ourselves with thinking this was something simply peculiar to the autistic child. From the point of view of our investigations, the problem of dimensionality was only a subsidiary feature of the autistic child that impeded his development. It didn't seem to be in any way the nuclear disturbance in the autistic child. It seemed to have something more to do with what we call dismantling—that is, really destroying the mind temporarily so that there was no possibility of functioning or not functioning.

Mrs Bick had already shown us the way, that this problem of containment was not simply something that she discovered operating in this terribly psychotic little girl that she had been treating all those years, but that it threw up phenomena that she recognised taking place in many other patients. Our eyes were opened, and we began to see evidences of what we are now calling "two-dimensionality"; that is, a tendency to relate to objects in the outside world as if they were flat or as if they were solid, as really only surfaces to relate to. They could possibly be burrowed into but only in the sense of finding a homogeneous substance inside them.

The main thing here is the relating to the surface and the surface qualities of the object. I think we began to see evidence of this in quite a few patients and evidence of mimicry operating in their relationship to the analyst in the transference. So it did open up a new area of phenomena for observation and also opened up to exploration certain categories of character difficulties which hadn't really attracted our attention as being distinct from other character difficulties. That, you might say, opened up a new way of viewing the general problem of what had for many years been called "ego strength". That is, it did seem to us that what Mrs Bick was discovering about containment and what we were discovering about two-dimensionality—the tendency to relate to surface qualities—played a very important part in the general problem of what had been lumped together under the title of ego strength, which seemed to me something like the general capacity to bear mental strain—not necessarily mental pain, and not necessarily persecution or depression, and not necessarily excluding physical illness or fatigue or intoxication or any sort of general stress. The problem that we were touching on related to containment of the self and having internal objects that could function as containers and seemed to give us a clue to the general problem of ego strength. It particularly opened our eyes to those phenomena in patients that Mrs Bick described as having sudden, rather inexplicable types of collapse—collapse into exhaustion, syndromes of a type Freud would have called neurasthenia, sudden needs for holidays, going to bed for a few days, urgently having to have a vacation, or rather, physical manifestations such as vomiting on the street, having sudden nosebleeds, runny noses, and crying.

Accompanying this two-dimensionality that was related to the tendency of adhesive identification to the surface qualities of objects, we also discovered that there was a certain flatness or thinness of affect that related to that particular sphere of the personality. I remember a patient of mine whose husband was always complaining that she was always sitting behind *The Times*—reading the newspaper—but in fact she wasn't reading the newspaper. She was "looking at" the newspaper. That is, she was sitting with a newspaper in front of her. And she didn't actually read it with a sense of comprehending the meaning of it. She just went through it, went through it column by column, reading the words but not taking in the meaning at all. This was her form of relaxation. That would seem to be a good illustration of what I mean by a kind of thinness of affect. Of relating oneself *to* something but not to the *meaning* of it. Only to its surface qualities which of course in the case of reading means reading the words but not reading the meaning of the sentence and not taking in the significance of the paragraph.

Now this kind of thinking was happening about the time that Dr Bion's series of books was coming out; *Learning from Experience* had already come out and had influenced us greatly. *The Elements of Psychoanalysis* had come out and knocked us all down, as it were, and it took us years to begin to grasp what in the world he was talking about. *Transformations* was even more traumatic. I must say, it has taken me many years to discover the tremendous impact those books had on me.

It was really only when I undertook to teach a course at the Tavistock Clinic on Dr Bion's work and was absolutely forced to transform what I thought I understood about it into actual knowledge about what I thought I understood and to put it into words for other people that I began to grasp what a tremendous influence it had had on my thinking. And, of course, what is central to Dr Bion's ideas are these concepts of container and contained which link so much to our work with autistic children and to Mrs Bick's work. And then, of course, Bion's incredible step forward into a real theory of thinking for the first time, I think, in psychoanalysis: the theory of alpha function and the Grid.

This evening I want to try to discuss with you a bit more this business about meaning. And perhaps one of the most useful ways to do it would be to tell you some material from a child whose analysis I supervised who has made the most intelligent, systematic, relentless, and fascinating attack on the meaningfulness of the relationship between himself and his analyst that I have ever seen. I think in seeing the ways in which he has gone about destroying the meaning of the relationship one can perhaps get some idea, by turning it on its head, what the meaning of the meaning is. So let's see if I can describe this little boy to you.

He's a little boy who is now seven, I suppose. He was a quite severely autistic child when he first came into analysis at about the age of three, three and a half. I remember he was treated for the first year and a half by a clinician who then asked me for supervision the last year of his analysis. In the early days his autism manifested itself in mutism, in being totally uneducable and unmanageable, and in what was called by his family "dervishing". He was continually whirling about, whirling about and ricocheting off objects in a sort of continual activity. His therapist agonised over him for about a year and a half, and the latter months of treatment turned into a crisis of separation between the two of them. This made a dramatic turning point in the child's development. By the time he started a subsequent treatment with a new therapist, which has now gone on for two years, he had absorbed the impact of his first therapist really going away, which had been unthinkable to him, not unthinkable so much as a laceration to his heart, but as a breach of his omnipotent control and also a laceration to his feeling.

The boy's material just began to blossom, and pictures began to pour out of him. His play, however, was very repetitive; session after session it was almost always the same, but each session had little modifications. Then he went through quite a long period of being very preoccupied, as he had started to be with the first therapist, about trains. With her he had been preoccupied primarily with the underground that he took from his home to the clinic and to a very great extent with the advertisements along the escalators going up and down at the tube station— many of which were young women in bikini bathing suits. But now in treatment he was very preoccupied with trains, trains passing through a landscape, and a landscape that had a bridge and a volcano. This bridge and volcano and sun and the position of the child in the train was a repetitive theme, and the most important element of it was the danger of passing over the bridge and the noises coming from the volcano. There didn't seem to be a danger of eruption, lava, and so forth, but noises—very frightening noises—coming from the volcano.

This theme of the frightening noises gradually developed into a theme of the boy's being terribly noisy and abusive and obscene in his language but at the same time being very frightened of its being heard, overheard by anybody who might be at the door, or particularly by his father who was in the waiting room. And that seemed to be the anxiety situation that crystallised to which he could find no solution. His demands of the therapist took the form that she mustn't have any other children in treatment but himself (she must not have any other babies), that she must undress and show herself naked to him, and that she must have no holidays. In relation to these demands and her refusal to acquiesce to these demands, his outbursts of verbal abuse, then the anxiety that they would be overheard, he began systematically to try to attack the meaningfulness of their relationship. And this he represented by attacks on the materials with which he had made his original drawings, particularly the felt-tip pens. He made systematic attacks to destroy the felt-tip pens, but it wasn't simply a matter of destroying the pens and therefore destroying the capacity to make pictures that would represent the meaning. The point was to destroy the meaning of the felt-tip pens. And this he did by a series of debates in which he demonstrated, or insisted that he could demonstrate to his therapist, that no matter how destroyed a felt-tip pen was, if any shred of it could still be said to contain a shred of felt-tip pen-ish-ness, you might say, then nothing had been destroyed; nothing had been wasted.

The approach that his therapist made to this was an approach that took the problem out of the realm of felt-tip pens and felt-tip pen-ish-ness, and whether a little shred of felt could still be called a felt-tip pen. She lifted it out of that realm and brought it into the realm of the question of her interest and her attention and her mental states; particularly about the time of her life and whether or not he could defend himself against the charge of wasting the time of her life, wasting her patience and interest, and possibly bringing the therapy to a point where her interest and patience could be exhausted. This had a very great impact on him, but the result of it was that a whole new operation started. He began to bring things into the session which he had scavenged in forays with his father to a nearby rubbish dump or something of the sort. He began to bring in little bits and pieces of musical instruments, radios, and televisions. And it began to reverse the process that had been represented by the destruction of the felt-tip pens; that is, he began to bring in debris of what you might call music-making apparatus with the avowed intention of constructing for himself from this debris a talking machine to replace his therapist.

At that time his therapist interpreted to him and examined with him whether or not his proposed construction could really substitute for her, and whether it was really possible that he preferred a machine—particularly a machine that didn't work. There had never been an assertion on his part that the device would work, but that it would simply be enough for him that it would represent a substitute for her. When she methodically challenged his assertion that this would be an adequate substitute because this meant that he would really prefer a non-working, ugly assemblage of debris that he called a talking machine to herself as his therapist, another level of phenomena appeared. He began to construct in phantasy a modification of the room; there was a sort of protective plastic sheeting going up to about four feet on the walls, and it was held in place by a kind of beading which in turn was held in place by screws. This beading and the screws were said by him to be a public address system leading from the consulting room into the waiting room where his father would be waiting. And these screws were filters which he could adjust so that he could abuse her to his heart's content, but what his father would hear in the waiting room would be only sweet sounds and sweet, inoffensive words.

His preoccupation started out with the danger of this volcano rumbling and making frightening sounds that were connected with his abuse of his therapist when she wouldn't acquiesce to his possessive and erotic and sensuous demands of her. He ended up with a system that was intended to enable him to abuse her without, you might say, the volcano knowing about it and by means of this apparatus which filtered out the truth and delivered into the waiting room a pack of lies. But nonetheless, it was still allowing meaning to flow even if the meaning was being so filtered that what got through was like the censorship of the news. The impression at the end of the censorship was entirely different from the impression of the full news story before it had been censored. But still, meaning had been re-established.

So there was first the period of attempting to destroy the meaning and significance of his relationship with her by these very cynical devices using and misusing words to prove that words were meaningless. For instance, the little shred of felt *was* a felt tipped pen and therefore nothing should be wasted, and therefore there was no such thing as waste, and then swinging over into the other attack on meaning; that pieces of debris, because they originally came from things that had to do with music, could really be called a musical instrument or a talking machine and that that was just as good as, if not better than, a human being to relate to. There were these two attacks on meaning; one an attack that said that meaning doesn't exist, and the other attack that said meaning can be created ad lib in any way you please. That little boy seemed to me to make a very strong link to Dr Bion's work, on the one hand, with the concept of the beta screen, the idea of alpha function working in reverse, and the idea, which hadn't yet been completely developed, of the negative Grid. But what it also linked with was this little boy's very beginnings as an autistic child and the world of meaninglessness where only surface qualities exist.

Projective identification, dimensionality, and delusional systems

Mrs Klein described projective identification as a general phenomenon. You could easily have described all sorts of different forms of narcissistic identification as they existed in hypochondria, as they existed in claustrophobia; you could have had hypochondriac identification, claustrophobic identification, confusional identification, and so on. I suppose the stroke of genius in this field partly relates to the ability to see what was the selected fact—the most general organising principle. It would seem to me that the general differentiation between object-related identifications and narcissistic identifications would be the top level of our generalising; we generally think that the object-related identifications are essentially introjective and occur primarily with internalised objects. That may be wrong. There may be other aspects of object-related identifications that haven't yet been described. We assumed for a long time that projective identification *was* narcissistic identification. Well, now there's a second form. So that you have to put these two under the general heading of narcissistic identification. We might discover a third or fourth. And then under projective identification, one could easily describe subcategories of projective identifications, as I did last night in describing the spaces inside the mother's body and the different mental states that relate to these subspaces, and so on. You could probably do the same with adhesive identification.

The question of introjective identification isn't really something I'm able to get to at this point, but I hope to get to it much later—though perhaps it is worthwhile talking about now. I mean, I don't think that adhesive identifications or introjective identifications have anything to do with swallowing. I think that introjective identification is something that comes about in a most mysterious way through an intensely cooperative relationship between an object that wishes to project and an object that wishes to accept the projection. It's not only the baby that introjects from the breast, it's also the mother who introjects the baby: not simply accepts the projection of distressed parts of the self as Dr Bion has described in order to return them to the baby in a less distressed state. But the mother does also introject the baby as a person in her internal world and the baby introjects from the mother not simply a breast or nipple and not simply a mother, but introjects what the mother wishes to project into the baby which generally we assume is a mother and father, a united couple, a combined object. It isn't much related to swallowing and different kinds of swallowing or cannibalistic internalisations, as it used to be called. It seems to me that introjection is a much more mysterious mind-to-mind process which may go on and perhaps optimally does go on in the infant–breast relationship; that is, the infant–mother relationship at the moment when the mother is feeding the infant with the breast—the baby is getting its nourishment from the breast. The introjective processes are mind-to-mind processes.

It seems to me that at present, in tracing the consequences of the operation of these modes of relationship that we call introjection, projective identification, and so on, our tendency is to try to examine them on the basis of their relationship to two different spectra that have to do with the mode of operation of these mechanisms. One is the spectrum from sadism to love and the other is the spectrum from, you might say, intense omnipotence to humility. We do, in fact, examine the consequences of these operations—of these mechanisms—as to the degree of sadism and the degree of omnipotence with which they are implemented, because they certainly have very different consequences.

In the actual clinical situation, classification is one that derives from the descriptive names as they appear in the patient's dreams, the patient's anecdotal associations, by which you come to have terms of reference that you and the patient agree upon for designating particular phantasy constellations. But that isn't of any use pedagogically. The kind of classification that I tend to use is the classification of geographical spaces and the classification of the splitting of the infantile self into various generally recognisable parts—the baby, little boy, little girl, destructive part of the self, and so on. And that seems to me to be enough to get on with pedagogically in terms of doing supervision of other people's work. There's something always to be lost in classifying too. You know, it's the story that Dr Bion speaks of about the container and the question of its being either incontinent or so rigid that it squeezes the meaning. Classifications have a very great tendency to squeeze the meaning.

In talking about two-dimensionality it's true, as in the patient described by Mrs Bick, that it is very common in patients who have a leaky containment. The point about two-dimensionality is that it relates to the object quite outside the sphere of containment. Two-dimensionality can function as a defensive position, you might say, rather than as a specific defence against anxiety. It is equivalent to what in war communiqués used to be called "withdrawing to a more strategic position". That's not the same as defending yourself against the enemy. It's a euphemism for retreating, and I certainly have seen two-dimensionality to be a position to which people retreat at a moment when they are threatened with panicky affect. That doesn't make it a mechanism of defence.

Dismantling is quite a different thing. In the autism book, I tried to relate it to certain aspects of fetishism and to the so-called transitional objects and to certain aspects of obsessionality in general. This is a dismantling of the sensory apparatus insofar as it is, most of the time, automatically treated in what Dr Bion calls a common sense way, or what Harry Stack Sullivan called "consensuality". Dismantling is the dismantling of that consensuality into discrete sensory modes of perception and relationship to the world, and it's something quite different from two-dimensionality as we were seeing it and describing it.

We thought in the autistic children that dismantling was very clearly a flight from overwhelming depressive anxiety impinging on an as-yet extremely primitive personality structure. I would say it was a flight rather than a defence. You see, one of the things that you have to consider is the problem of the sense of identity, so that what presents itself to you in the consulting room at any moment is really that part of the personality that is, you might say, in possession of the organ of consciousness; that organ for the perception of psychic qualities, the possession of which carries with it a sense of identity. That I, at that particular moment, am that part of myself that is in possession of my organ of consciousness.

Now what happens, which you see most obtrusively in adolescence, is that different parts of the self which are split from one another come into possession of that organ of consciousness from moment to moment, day to day; it's as if you are talking to a different person who hardly remembers what happened yesterday. Well, the same thing happens in many flights from pain that don't really constitute a regression in the sense of a loss of organisation of the structure of the personality; that more primitive parts of the personality are allowed to take over this organ of consciousness and the sense of identity and to use their particular modes of relating to the world and to relate to the world that they experience.

A patient may shift from three- to two-dimensionality, from four- to three- to two-dimensionality, by shifting the contact that you're making in the transference with different parts of the personality without any regression taking place at all. And therefore, it isn't really correct, I think, in terms of theory, to call it either regression or a mechanism of defence. It is really a shift of the point of contact with the personality—that is, the point of contact offered to the world at that particular moment.

One can sometimes see adhesive identification, projective identification, and introjective identification operating in sequence in a single patient. I heard in a supervision today about a patient who at first was quite clearly presenting two-dimensional material and then suddenly shifted over into three-dimensional material about the babies inside the mother. It ended up with a yearning for a good father that he could identify with, who would refurbish this mother and bring her babies back to life so he wouldn't have to be out on the snowy slope. I mean, I absolutely saw the material shift from two- to three-dimensionality to introjective identification. And I would think that good sessions often can be traced in quite a different way from the sort of sequence that I demonstrated in *The Psycho-Analytical Process* which was really a cycle of object relationships at a three-dimensional and possibly four-dimensional level. With patients who have two-dimensional tendencies, you can see within a single session the cycle of dimensionality.

Now in the child we've been discussing, I think the level of dimensionality is motivated by a very powerful and despairing refusal of a relationship that is going to come to an end. It's the sort of thing that Mrs Bick calls "the dead end"—the fear of continuous falling and things of that sort. I would think that in this child, it may be in many ways similar to what Mrs Bick refers to as catastrophic anxiety, but I think that term doesn't quite catch the depressive quality of what I think this child is defending against, which he got a real whiff of at the ending of his therapy with his first therapist.

We take it that one-dimensionality is linear and is equivalent to a concept of tropism; that the impulse has only direction. By two-dimensionality we mean the experience of an object as at least a surface that has form and quality towards which the impulse may have not only direction but configuration. Three-dimensionality includes the possibility of spaces; that the object is three-dimensional and may have a space inside itself, and therefore a space outside, which is different from the internal space. And by four-dimensionality we mean another dimension of linear time is included, whereas in these other forms of dimensionality time is not apprehended as a linear process or a linear dimension. It's apprehended either as oscillating or circular or is non-existent.

It's rather interesting about this little boy. I described to you that one of his chief manifestations when he first came to therapy was what his family called his dervishing. When he came to make these attacks on meaning and carried out these lengthy Socratic debates with his therapist about the meaning of things, when she began to get through to him, he came to refer to those operations as his mind dervishing. This child, like most children who are well contained and in analysis, was tremendously improved and was able to go to school and start his learning. The kind of behaviour he was manifesting at the start of his treatment tended only to erupt a bit after weekends and holidays at home. It's a pretty ordinary picture that, as the transference relationship in an analysis deepens and becomes more infantile and more primitively disturbed, the child, or adult patient for that matter, begins to lead a much less troubled life outside. Of course one of the pitfalls of analytic therapy in a naïve community is that the parents often think the children are well and want to take them out of treatment prematurely.

This isn't a matter of the analyst getting the bad and the parents getting the good. This is a matter of the analyst getting the infantile and the primitive, and the parents getting the more mature aspect of the personality. There are those problems in therapy where an idealisation occurs and blankets the procedures in an analysis, and all the bad is split off and acted out with the parents or at school. Or conversely, where a negative transference unrelentingly goes on and all the idealisation goes out to some teacher or aunt or someone like that. What I'm describing is a situation in which both the positive and negative transference are pretty well held together in the therapy at a very infantile level, and what the parents are getting at home is a far more sane and mature little boy who is beginning to be able to go to school and be able to learn to read and write.

Now before we end, I'd like to say something about delusional ideas and delusional systems. I think we need to be able to conceptualise and find a way to describe the difference between the two.

What I have described to you about delusional systems was in one way very similar to what Freud described in the Schreber case, but also an extension of his description in two ways. One is that I suggested that every person has a delusional system that is developed in parallel with the construction of his internal world and is constructed along the basis of a law of negativism, you might say. Anti-nature. That is constructed by the most destructive satanic part of the personality, and I have equated it with Milton's description of Satan building pandemonium. The patient, or the part of the personality that is tempted to enter into that delusional system, is tempted (speaking in geographical terms) into a place that is beyond the gravitational pull of the beauty and goodness of the world. The fear of becoming schizophrenic is often experienced by patients as a fear of just floating into space. The patient quite often fears the return of the schizophrenic parts of the self and of being invaded and overwhelmed by parts of themselves that have disappeared into the extra-global interstellar spaces of the mind that have as their chief geographical characteristic a navigational nowhere.

Delusional ideas are very complicated because you have to consider delusional ideas (now that we have Dr Bion's Grid) from many different points of view. We even have to add to Dr Bion's Grid, Mr Money-Kyrle's idea of misconceptions, which are different from lies and different from cynical distortions of the truth. Delusional ideas seem to me in general not to fit in what Dr Bion has described as Column 2 in his Grid; that is, ideas that are known to be false but which are asserted as a defence against experiencing the truth. I don't think delusional ideas fit into what he describes as beta elements and beta screens. That is, the emotional experiences which have not been worked upon by alpha function in a way that creates symbols, enables dream formation, and so on. I think that delusional ideas as we encounter them clinically are part of the phenomenology of narcissism and relate specifically to these processes we've been talking about tonight connected with narcissistic identification processes. That is, projective and adhesive identification processes. I think there are other aspects of narcissism that have to do with splitting processes and with narcissistic organisations, gang formation, and so on that don't get into the realm of delusional ideas. But the distortions of the world imposed by these changes of the geography brought about by projective or adhesive types of identification do seem to me to generate what we generally call delusional ideas. But then, delusional ideas of this sort are Dr Bion's Row C and can be elevated to higher levels of abstraction and become the most sophisticated delusional scientific systems. Milton's theology, for instance, was probably at the same level of abstraction as the infinitesimal calculus, but on a delusional level.

The apprehension of time as a linear dimension and function seems to me from the emotional point of view to be an extremely sophisticated realisation because it has to do with actually acknowledging a beginning and an end to the self as individual. Generally, what we have to take its place is the apparent circularity of time, of day and night, of the seasons, and so on. But that doesn't really go anywhere. And patients who employ projective identification a great deal experience time changes related to going in and out of their objects, as if it were equivalent to reversible time, to being able to go backwards in time and forwards in time and backwards in time and forwards in time, as if time were simply an oscillating system and could be reversed at a moment's notice. So, I think I will stop here and take a few questions.

Part II

Selected papers by founding members of The Psychoanalytic Center of California

CHAPTER 6

Projective identification
in the therapeutic process*

Arthur Malin and James S. Grotstein

R ecent articles by Loewald (1960) and Searles (1963) having to do
with certain aspects of the therapeutic process have stimulated
us to investigate what we believe may be the basis of the therapeutic effect in psychoanalysis. In our view the concept of projective
identification can be fruitfully applied to an understanding of the therapeutic process. We shall attempt to describe the concept of projective
identification and then discuss the relevance of this idea to normal and
pathological development with a view towards clarifying the therapeutic process in light of it.

The term projective identification was first used by Melanie Klein
(1946) and was meant to indicate a process in which parts of the self
are split off and projected into an external object or part object. Hanna
Segal (1964) states,

---

* Presented to the Los Angeles Psychoanalytic Society, September 16, 1965. This paper
was first published in 1966 in the *International Journal of Psychoanalysis 47*: 26–31,
copyright © Institute of Psychoanalysis reprinted by permission of Taylor & Francis
Ltd, http://www.tandfonline.com on behalf of Institute of Psychoanalysis.

> Projective identification is the result of the projection of parts
> of the self into an object. It may result in the object's being per-
> ceived as having acquired the characteristics of the projected
> part of the self, but it can also result in the self becoming identi-
> fied with the object of its projection.

This idea was developed from Klein's (1932, 1934) earlier concept of
object relations existing from the start of extrauterine life. Klein had
indicated that the relation to the first object, the breast, is through
introjection.[1] She also demonstrated that object relations from the
beginning depend for their development on projective and introjective
mechanisms. Klein (1946) suggested that these mechanisms are seen in
the earliest period of normal development, which she described as the
paranoid–schizoid position. She stated further that these mechanisms
are also a type of defence found particularly in schizophrenic patients.

We wish to emphasise at this point that projective identification to us
has come to mean many different things and embraces many concepts.
Our paper is an attempt, both to clarify and to expand on it, and to
place it in its proper perspective in psychoanalytic theory and practice.

First, we should like to say why we use the term projective identification and not projection. Projection alone is a mechanism for dealing
with instinctual drives, akin to incorporation. It is an instinctual mode.
We feel, as does Fairbairn (1952), that all intraphysic and interpersonal
relations are transacted on the basis of object relationships, rather than
on the basis of instinctual drives alone. The object is the irreducible
vehicle in human interaction.

Once we make this assumption, we then conceive of the psychic
apparatus as a dynamic structure composed of internalised objects (and
part objects) with drive charges inseparably attached to them. We feel
that these charged parts of self (or identifications) are projected out-
ward and that the status of the identification changes by virtue of the

---

[1] We define introjection as a psychic phenomenon in which the object is taken into the
psychic apparatus but is kept separate from the self; in other words, it is within the
ego but unassimilated, much like a foreign body. Following introjection, identification
may take place by the object's becoming assimilated into the ego or self. See Greenson
(1954).

projection, thus enabling the ego to discharge, for instance, unwanted or disclaimed parts of the self (purified pleasure ego of Freud, 1915c). The external object now receives the projected parts, and then this alloy—external object plus newly arrived projected part—is re-introjected to complete the cycle.

In the preceding paragraph, we have dealt with the defensive nature of projective identification. We wish to emphasise that it is also, at the same time, a way of relating to objects. As Freud (1921c) has stated, the infant relates by identification prior to making anaclitic object choices. We agree with this and go two steps further; first, we believe that all identification includes projection, as we hope to show; and second, that projective identification is also a normal, as well as abnormal, way of relating which persists into mature adulthood.[2]

We hope to develop the reasons why these burdensome emendations of theory are necessary, especially since the advent of object relations theory has imposed this task upon us.

An article by Knight (1940) appears to anticipate the concept of projective identification although it is not described directly by that name. In this short article Knight attempts to describe the different ways in which identification may be used and defined. Knight states,

> identification is never an irreducible process or state of affairs, but is always based on a subtle interaction of both introjective and projective mechanisms.

Knight makes a point that Bibring's term, "altruistic surrender", involves a projection of one's own desires for pleasure and gratification into another person with whom one then identifies. Knight goes further and states,

> The awareness of how we would feel under similar circumstances enables us to project our own needs and wishes on to the object and then to experience his feelings as if they were ours through the resultant temporary identification with him. Even though

---

[2] Erikson (1959) has shown that the mother also projects her needs and feelings into the infant and responds to the child's perception of these needs.

this vicarious experience would appear to be an instantaneous process, it seems to me valuable to reduce it to its constituent mechanisms of projection and possibly also introjection.

It is obvious that Knight is referring to identification with whole objects rather than part objects as emphasised by Klein, but Knight's ideas are certainly compatible with the concept of projective identification.

In line with Knight's thinking, we want to emphasise what seems obvious in the concept of identification, namely, that all identification includes projection, and all projection includes identification.[3] Before we are ready to internalise (take in psychically, incorporate), we must be in some state of readiness for this process. That is, we must tentatively project out a part of our inner psychic contents in order to be receptive to the object for introjection and subsequently to form an identification with it. When we start with the projection it is necessary that there be some process of identification or internalisation in general, or else we can never be aware of the projection. That is, what is projected would be lost like a satellite rocketed out of the gravitational pull of the Earth. Eventually all contact with the satellite will be lost. Although the satellite has left Earth, it must remain under the influence of Earth's gravitational pull to remain in orbit in order for it to maintain some contact with Earth. A projection, of itself, seems meaningless unless the individual can retain some contact with what is projected. That contact is a type of internalisation, or, loosely, an identification. We want to show that Klein's concept of projective identification can be broadened greatly in order to understand many phenomena in psychic life both normal and pathological, and to enhance our knowledge of identification itself.

Rosenfeld (1952a, 1952b, 1954) and Bion (1955, 1956) have applied the concept of projective identification to the understanding and treatment of the psychotic patient. They state that when a patient splits off a part of himself and projects it into the object, such as the analyst, he has

---

[3] We define introjection as a psychic phenomenon in which the object is taken into the psychic apparatus but is kept separate from the self; in other words, it is within the ego but unassimilated, much like a foreign body. Following introjection, identification may take place by the object's becoming assimilated into the ego or self. See Greenson (1954).

a feeling of relatedness to the analyst but with some corresponding feelings of inner impoverishment. Very often the patient feels that the split-off part, now in the external object, is a persecutor. They emphasise the importance of projective identification in understanding delusional transference material.

Searles (1963) describes very similar phenomena. He relates much of his material to the Kleinian concept of projective identification, but he does emphasise some important differences between his ideas and Klein's. In a more broadly defined manner, however, we would view Searles's ideas on transference psychosis as being another aspect of projective identification. Searles makes an important point, for instance, of the schizophrenic patient's need to project a part of himself into the therapist. The therapist must provide, according to Searles, a suitable and receptive object in himself to receive this projection from the patient. Searles suggests,

> Moreover, it is my experience that he [the chronic schizophrenic patient] actively needs a degree of symbiotic relatedness in the transference, which would be interfered with were the analyst to try, recurrently, to establish with him the validity of verbalized transference interpretations.

Searles suggests here that the projective identification from the patient to the analyst must first be accepted by the analyst before verbal interpretations will be of any help.

Loewald (1960) writes of therapeutic change as involving structural change in the ego. In speaking of the patient's reaction to the analyst, Loewald states,

> A higher stage of organization, of both himself and his environment, is thus reached, by way of the organizing understanding which the analyst provides.

Loewald emphasises throughout his article the importance of higher levels of ego integration which the patient can achieve through the analytic treatment. We suggest that projective identification helps explain the development of these higher levels of ego integration.

Transference phenomena are obviously very closely related to projective identification. Transference implies the projection of inner attitudes which came from earlier object relationships into the figure of the analyst during the analysis. A much broader concept of transference would state that all subsequent relationships are modified on the basis of the earliest object relationship of the individual which is now established in the inner psychic life. This view very closely approximates the concept of primary objects which was advanced by Balint (1937). If we accept a broad view of transference to include all object relations, internal and external, after the primary relationship with the breast-mother which is now internalised, then we are stating that all object relations and all transference phenomena are examples, at least in part, of projective identification. This implies that there must be a projection from within the psychic apparatus into the external object. We emphasise that this includes parts of self as well as internal object representations. To go back to Klein's ideas for a moment, some of her lack of emphasis on the environment in human development can be understood in terms of projective identification. It can be understood in the sense that the early instinctual representations, including the death instinct, are projected into the breast-mother, and then the bad breast-mother is introjected on the basis of the earlier projection and not so much on the basis of the actual environmental situation of that breast-mother. We should like to modify this idea, however, with the suggestion that it is just the fact that the inner psychic contents related to earliest object relations are projected into the external objects that makes for the tremendous influence of the environment. *It seems to us that it is only upon perceiving how the external object receives our projection and deals with our projection that we now introject back into the psychic apparatus the original projection, but now modified and on a newer level.* Hopefully, the mother has helped the infant by allowing this projection to be met with a response of understanding, care, and love. It is the mother who cannot do this, and who sees the child's projections as destructive and frightening, who will confirm the infant's fears of his own bad destructive self.[4] We suggest, moreover, that this method of projecting one's inner psychic

---

[4] Erikson (1959) has shown that the mother also projects her needs and feelings into the infant and responds to the child's perception of these needs.

contents into external objects and then perceiving the response of these external objects and introjecting this response on a new level of integration is the way in which the human organism grows psychically, nurtured by his environment. The environment must meet the needs of these projections and be able to reinterpret for the developing individual the inner workings of their psychic apparatus and to demonstrate that these are not destructive, "bad" parts. The external object must confirm those constructive and "good" aspects of the developing individual and thus facilitate higher ego integration which will mitigate the effect of the destructive components of the self.

We propose that these concepts are of crucial importance in understanding the earliest experiences of the infant, the further growth and development of children and adults, and to a great extent the therapeutic effect of psychoanalysis. We have all observed how patients must project into the analyst their inner psychic contents. These consist of objects and part objects with associated feelings and attitudes. It is mainly through his perception of the manner in which the analyst handles these projections that the patient can find a new level of integration. As Searles (1963) emphasises, what is important is a receptiveness without an encouragement of these projections, and an attempt at understanding their meaning without the fear that these projections will destroy the analyst.

The essence of the therapeutic process is through modification of internal object relationships within the ego, and this is largely brought about by projective identification. Correct interpretations can be seen as an important way in which the patient can observe how his projections have been received and acknowledged by the analyst. If this does not take place the patient is left with futility, despair, and doubt in regard to his inner self worth.

One of the most common defences of the schizophrenic borderline patient, as well as of many neurotics, is the need to preserve the analyst as a good object by maintaining a distance which paradoxically is not very helpful to developing understanding. Much of this is related to what seems to be a negative therapeutic reaction. It would appear that these patients are trying to preserve the analyst by avoiding closeness to him, that is, not projecting any of their bad parts into the analyst which they feel will destroy the analyst and therefore their only hope for survival. For example, a borderline patient could rarely speak of any positive feelings towards the analyst, but would occasionally, with great disappointment, point out what he felt was an error on the part of the analyst. It was learned in the analysis that in this way the patient would demonstrate his great reliance and positive attitude towards the analyst, but only through this method of expressing disappointment. To speak directly of his concern and closeness to the analyst would be forbidden because the patient felt that any closeness and trust would mean that the analyst would have to handle the patient's destructiveness and would therefore be destroyed. Therefore, to keep some distance from the analyst was to preserve him. Conversely, a patient may often keep his distance because he has already projected bad objects into the analyst and therefore sees the analyst as a persecutor.

The following case history will illustrate some of the above ideas. A twenty-three-year-old civil engineer came into analysis because of increasing anxiety over his loneliness. He found himself very aloof from his fellow office workers towards whom he felt a mixture of fear and contempt and did not dare, as a consequence, get close to them. His sexual life, other than masturbation, consisted of a few contacts with prostitutes and one contact with a girl towards whom he had begun to develop feelings. Subsequent sexual attempts with her resulted in humiliating impotent failures, however, so he abruptly terminated the relationship with her. His life otherwise was characterised by a lonely, stark impoverishment in which he spent most of his spare time in his apartment, drinking, playing the guitar, or reading.

He was the second eldest of four children, having an older sister and a younger brother and sister respectively. His father was described as an angry, loud, drunk, martinet of a man who once was a prizefighter. His mother was a willowy, soft-spoken, subtly patronising martyr of a woman who was frequently beaten by the father while the children watched in paralysed horror. When the patient was twelve, the mother "escaped" from the father and encouraged her children to come with her. Only the oldest child obliged, however; the others remained with the father. Immediately thereafter the father moved them away from New York to a small town in California where he forced them to use assumed names so that the mother could not trace them and have them brought back to New York.

Life with father consisted of hearing his insults and temper fits, sub-jecting oneself to Spartan discipline (the father enforced regular calis-thenics upon them as if they were in training), and consistently being reminded of what a better parent he was than their mother who, he claimed, wanted them sent to an orphans' home. After graduating from high school the patient left home against his father's will and used his savings to enter college to become an engineer.

His initial behaviour in analysis was cold, formal, and detached. He would describe a very lonely, impoverished life with an eerie detach-ment. He did not seem to be involved with his own life. Provocative gestures at work, such as frequently arriving late, allowing himself to be seen idle, and arguments with the supervisor, changed into transfer-ence phenomena of professing mild to enormous contempt and ridicule towards the analyst, whose weaknesses and deficiencies almost invari-ably bore a striking resemblance to the patient's own shortcomings, in addition to shortcomings of both parents. Examples of some of the pro-jections are as follows: frequently he would accuse the analyst of being weak and poorly integrated and possibly suffering from a huge inner impoverishment. Along with this he would state that he felt the analyst also had a hidden homosexual problem. These all were projections of his weak self-concept. On other occasions he would berate the analyst as being too rigid and demanding, and he would freely express how he hated pleasing him—that would be like giving in. This perception of the analyst as rigid, autocratic, and hard to please, represented a projection of the father identification. On still other occasions he would perceive the analyst as supercilious, polite, ingratiating, insincere, and martyr-like. All these qualities belonged to his mother identification.

The projections were accepted by the analyst for their psychic valid-ity, and then interpreted as his need to put bad parts of himself, includ-ing bad objects and part objects, into the analyst in order to rid his ego of these bad contents. In addition he was symbolically entering the analyst through these projections, to take control of him by weakening his self-esteem through consistent criticism and denigration. Not only was he repeating with the analyst what he had experienced with his father and mother, but he was also taking possession, in fantasy, of the analyst from within to guarantee total possession of the object. In his life history there was no precedent for him to assume he could have any relationship with anyone without total control or total subjugation. Without this guarantee, as it were, there existed no relationship for him.

The projection of bad parts of himself (and bad objects and part objects) had still another purpose which closely dovetailed with the mechanisms described. This patient was so trapped in his schizoid world that he could not trust his good, positive love feelings to be truly good. He had the conviction that his very love was bad and would be rejected; thus he related with his overtly bad self in order to establish a relationship and, paradoxically, protect the external object and himself from destruction. Moreover, he got a particular delight if he felt the analyst was hurt by his tirades of abuse. As long as the analyst was hurt (i.e. affected), then he as an individual was having some effect on another person and was therefore asserting his identity and was at the same time dealing with his deep envy of the analyst's immutability.

Consistent interpretations of all of these mechanisms wherever they occurred considerably lessened the negative transference, and the patient was subsequently able to recognise that he was warding off his deep feelings of dependency on the analyst. Changes occurred by virtue of analysing the projections rather than by the analyst's unconsciously or consciously responding as if they were objectively valid. In other words, this was a new experience for the patient which allowed him to integrate the previously projected parts, now reintegrated into the ego, so that a higher level of functioning could occur. This is an example of transference, but it is also something more than is ordinarily conveyed by that term. The patient was not merely displacing from the past; he was projecting from within himself bad contents into the analyst. By permitting the patient to project into the analyst, that is, to accept the psychic validity of the projection, a way of establishing a relationship with the patient was developed which allowed successful interpretation and resolution of this archaic way of relating. It also anticipated and precluded a negative therapeutic reaction and aided the patient to heal his ego fragments.

In the light of all the above material we should like to offer some speculative ideas in regard to the general concept of identification. We suggest the possibility that there is an early primary identification with the breast-mother and that in a sense no further real identification takes place. Instead, there is a constant modifying and integrating of this earliest identification. This might explain the contradiction that appears in the literature in regard to identification at one point appearing as a normal process of development and at another point as a pathological defence mechanism. It would seem that normal identification refers to the primary identification and that any further identification later on in life would be of a more pathological defensive nature more likely on the level of introjection, that is, an unassimilated foreign-body reaction in the psychic apparatus. However, normal development does include identification, but of a far more transient nature than originally assumed, which really has to do with further structuring, integrating, and synthesising of the earliest primary identification. What are commonly thought of as good identifications can be seen to be growth of the self through these mechanisms. It may be stated that we can never change the facts of what has happened to the patient in his life. What we hope to do, however, is to help the patient integrate his experiences in a new way so that he may have a choice in the way he relates to the world.[5]

Fairbairn (1952) has made an interesting contribution to the concept of identification. He feels that primary identification takes place with the pre-ambivalent object, which is then split into good and bad objects. All future identifications are made solely with the bad objects. The good objects, he states, do not need to be identified with. There is a different kind of internalising of the good objects, but this is transitory and is given up as one matures. In other words, the good objects are loosely held as a scaffolding, as it were, for ego growth and differentiation. As this takes place, the scaffolding is removed.

To summarise, we are suggesting that projective identification is a normal process existing from birth. It is one of the most important mechanisms by which growth and development take place through object relations. This mechanism can be described as one in which objects and associated affects are re-experienced on a new integrative level so that further synthesis and development will take place within the ego.

We have taken Klein's concept of projective identification and have attempted to show how this idea can be greatly broadened to increase our understanding of normal and pathological development and the therapeutic process. In our view projective identification seems to be

---

[5] See Lichtenstein's (1961) concept of "identity theme".

the way in which human beings are able to test their own inner psychic life by projecting psychic contents out into the environment and perceiving the environment's reaction to these projected parts of oneself. This process gives rise to newer psychic integrations leading to normal growth and development, and is, moreover, of crucial importance in the therapeutic process.

References

Balint, M. (1937). Early developmental states of the ego: primary object love. In: *Primary Love and Psychoanalytic Technique*. London: Hogarth, 1952.

Bion, W. R. (1955). Language and the schizophrenic. In: M. Klein, P. Heimann, & R. E. Money-Kyrle (Eds.), *New Directions in Psycho-Analysis*. London: Tavistock.

Bion, W. R. (1956). Development of schizophrenic thought. *International Journal of Psychoanalysis, 37*: 344–346.

Erikson, E. H. (1959). *Identity and the Life Cycle: Selected Papers*. Psychological Issues Monogr. 1. New York: International Universities Press.

Fairbairn, W. R. D. (1952). *Psychoanalytic Studies of the Personality*. London: Tavistock. American title: *An Object-Relations Theory of the Personality*. New York: Basic Books, 1954.

Freud, S. (1915c). Instincts and their vicissitudes. *S. E., 14*. London: Hogarth.

Freud, S. (1921c). *Group Psychology and the Analysis of the Ego. S. E., 18*. London: Hogarth.

Greenson, R. R. (1954). The struggle against identification. *Journal of the American Psychoanalytic Association, 2*: 200–217.

Klein, M. (1932). *The Psycho-Analysis of Children*. London: Hogarth, 1950.

Klein, M. (1934). A contribution to the psychogenesis of manic-depressive states. In: *Contributions to Psycho-Analysis, 1921–1945*. London: Hogarth, 1950.

Klein, M. (1946). Notes on some schizoid mechanisms. In: J. Riviere (Ed.), *Developments in Psycho-Analysis*. London: Hogarth, 1952.

Knight, R. P. (1940). Introjection, projection and identification. *Psychoanalytic Quarterly, 9*(3): 334–341.

Lichtenstein, H. (1961). Identity and sexuality: a study of their interrelationship in man. *Journal of the American Psychoanalytic Association, 9*: 179–260.

Loewald, H. W. (1960). On the therapeutic action of psycho-analysis. *International Journal of Psychoanalysis, 41*: 16–33.

Rosenfeld, H. (1952a). Notes on the psychoanalysis of the super-ego conflict of an acute schizophrenic patient. *International Journal of Psychoanalysis, 33*(2): 111–131.

Rosenfeld, H. (1952b). Transference-phenomena and transference-analysis in an acute catatonic schizophrenic patient. *International Journal of Psychoanalysis, 33*(4): 457–464.

Rosenfeld, H. (1954). Considerations regarding the psycho-analytic approach to acute and chronic schizophrenia. *International Journal of Psychoanalysis, 35*: 135–140.

Searles, H. F. (1963). Transference psychosis in the psychotherapy of chronic schizophrenia. *International Journal of Psychoanalysis, 44*: 249–281.

Segal, H. (1964). *Introduction to the Work of Melanie Klein*. London: Heinemann.

CHAPTER 7

Reflections on my analysis with Dr Bion

James A. Gooch

It has been over fifty years since my personal analysis with Wilfred Bion. My process with him has deeply affected my life as a husband and father as well as my professional work as a teacher and practising analyst treating children, adolescents, and adults. In the intervening years since terminating my treatment with Bion in 1976, I have given much thought to the style, timing, and content of his interpretations, what made his interventions unique, and how they came to make a difference to my internal and external worlds. This paper is an attempt to organise my thoughts in an effort to paint a picture of this relationship and reflect upon what I have learned as a result.

Bion, both in person and in his writings, was very sensitive to and thoughtful about practical psychoanalytic epistemology: ephemeralness, evanescence, unknown sense organs of psychic qualities, problems regarding psychic common sense (multiple vertices equivalent to an upgraded depressive position), correlation, and communication. Having been with Bion reminds me of what it was like as a growing boy with my paternal grandfather and his sensitivity and thoughtfulness about the sensual experiences of nature as I encountered them in exquisite detail with him on his beloved farm in Kentucky. He would call to my attention the sights and sounds, odours, tastes, textures, temperatures, and weights of everything we came across—comparing, contrasting, and marvelling at nature with heartfelt wonder. Our intimate encounters with natural life led me to explorations on my own and attempts to share them with anyone who seemed interested. And so it was with Bion in the realm of psyche and related soma during our psychoanalytic sessions together, and when I read his work to this day.

I had eight years of training analysis in the 1960s with a respectful, humane American analyst. I had benefited from it but somehow remained dissatisfied in my practice of analysis with my patients to the extent that I was thinking of giving up analysis and returning to my practice of medicine, which I had so enjoyed as a student and, briefly, in private practice. I felt I was not able to fully use my total experience as an analyst; I did not know how to utilise my own emotional and physical awareness when in session, nor afterwards reflecting upon sessions or discussing them with colleagues. When I took my observations to supervisors and peers during my training, these puzzling experiences of mine were attributed to countertransference dynamics that needed to be taken up in my own analysis. By implication, these reverberations were regarded as interferences in the analyses I was conducting. While I recognised that such emotional and physical experiences needed to be addressed in my own analysis, I also felt intuitively that they could be used somehow in my analytic work if I could only discover how. Other supervisors and colleagues were struggling with similar intuitions and were as much at a loss as I as to how to utilise their emotional and physical awareness with and about their analysands.

In my first analysis interpretations were often made about my omnipotence, but I do not remember any instances when interpretations were made about what that omnipotence was defending against. I was desperate for insight into why I might need my omnipotence, but no answers were forthcoming. Needless to say, this was a very painful and lonely period for me, and I can only credit enduring it to my fierce determination to become an analyst.

Eventually I went into analysis with Bion because I had found a stint of Kleinian supervision with Albert Mason very helpful, including the exploration of my own emotional experience with each analysand in question. At last I saw that there was a possibility of a kind of practice of analysis in which I could be more integrally grounded in my own emotional and physical experiences in the moment with my analysands, as I had been with my patients in the practice of medicine. Perhaps I would not have to abandon ten years of dedicated work, training, tens of thousands of dollars, and the emotional counterpart of this process in a futile investment. My wife Shirley and I had just bought a home and had recently had our third child. When I conveyed my intention to her of returning to analysis, dismayed yet still supportive, she exclaimed, "If you're crazy enough to think you can afford analysis now, you need it!"

Analysis with Bion was a very different experience, notwithstanding some features which had commonality with my first analysis. There were many interpretations about my omnipotence, but in a remarkably different way. Without exception, Bion would "guess" (his word) what the omnipotence was a defence against, always calling my attention to the evidence in the session that supported his conjecture. When no evidence was available to him, he would say something like:

> My experience is whenever a person is omnipotent, he or she is feeling helpless about something. Omnipotence seems to be a psychic reflex for surviving actual helplessness, as in infancy, senility, or extreme physical illness. But if used at any other time it can produce helplessness, since it is an illusion. Perhaps you have some idea of what may be making you feel helpless, so that you are reduced to omnipotence.

Invariably, I would then be able to identify that about which I was feeling helpless. Bion might also suggest guesses based on what he called "hunches", and I am confident that he was drawing evidence from his own emotional experience. I felt Bion was "with me", and my loneliness was much less intense. In time, I could hear and feel his emotionality as he interpreted (that is, "guessed") what I might be struggling to find access to and feel in the moment. He would point out that even though he rarely told me directly of his own emotional experience, I was likely to know a great deal about him based upon what he was and was not able to understand of me.

The theoretical understanding of psychoanalytic technique that I will now describe has grown mostly out of my experience as an analysand of Bion, a reader of Bion and others, and my own decades of experience as an analyst. In my view, a psychoanalytic interpretation is a mature, respectful, compassionate, disciplined, and educated guess; a hypothesis, a description in words (imbued with a sort of resonant musicality) that addresses the analysand's emotional experience in the moment. Stated theoretically, the analysand's psychoanalytic (psychic) objects, intuited by the analyst to be active in the moment but unnoticed by the analysand, are described in the interpretation. Psychic objects are ephemeral, evanescent, and only able to be observed privately by the individual. In fashioning an interpretation, the analyst uses his or her own psychoanalytic objects—also ephemeral, evanescent, and observable only by the analyst—as these are evoked and provoked by the analysand's communication and behaviour.

In Bion's model, psychical objects are composed of one or more psychical elements which are thought to be analogous to, but different from, physical objects composed of chemical elements. Psychic elements occupy a single box on the Grid, analogous to the chemical elements of the Periodic Table. Psychical objects (and elements), as they are available to both the analysand and the analyst, have dimensions in the domains of sense (Row B), myth (Row C), and passion (Row G). Sense refers to noticeable sensorial manifestations, myth to signal affects and symbolic manifestations, and passion to the empathic link. Similar psychical objects, experienced by both analysand and analyst, communicated by the former to the latter, produce the analyst's intuition of the analysand's experience. This is very similar, if not equivalent to, the baby's conveying to the mother by way of normal projective identification its incomprehensible experiences (beta elements). These beta elements are acted upon by maternal reverie (alpha function), thereby creating alpha elements that are returned via maternal or paternal ministrations, often including the spoken but incomprehensible word, while it is the accompanying music and dance that convey the comprehensible understanding to the baby of any age.

I would modify maternal reverie to parental reverie, including maternal and paternal reverie in mature, cooperative, respectful union, ministering to the baby. Mature, respectful compassion and discipline cooperate to form dream function alpha or parental reverie. When psychoanalysts' accurate verbal interpretations are made from the heart, utilising our own psychic objects, then our words, like the lyrics of a song, help us get the music and dance right. I am increasingly convinced that it is the music and dance of our interpretations that are transformative to the infantile aspects of our analysands.

Conducting an analysis with an absence of memory and desire greatly facilitates the observation of psychical objects by both analyst and analysand, as nightfall facilitates seeing the stars. The analyst needs to be under the aegis of this mature internal couple—mother and father—in communion with one another in relationship to the psychoanalytic objects being experienced by the parental alpha function in the analyst and the immature consciousness of the analysand. Such attuned empathic experience in turn allows for psychic growth (+Y) in both analyst and analysand. In *Learning from Experience* Bion proposes that, aside from physical ministrations to the baby, the mother shows her love through reverie, psychically (Bion, 1962, p. 36). I am suggesting that the analyst's main work is to make this internal mother and father in communion available to the analysand. I believe the mature internal parental couple in the analyst is the psychoanalyst's primary instrument in attending to and analysing the unborn, immature, autistic, somatised, psychotic, criminal, perverse, and otherwise pathologic and pathogenic aspects of our analysands. Such *in vivo* parental alpha function shows the analysand how the intolerable, toxic, undigested experiences (beta elements) can be tolerated (detoxified, digested). Through the mysterious process of introjective identification in a mature K link between analyst and analysand, the analysand develops a capacity that he or she did not previously possess—that is, the capacity for meaningful emotional experience.

Much as physical exercise and athletic conditioning facilitate learning a physical skill, so psychical exercise develops psychical skills. I sometimes refer to this as the development of mental muscle. In particular, this psychical exercise develops dream function alpha and the alpha membrane. Bion, in *Learning from Experience*, uses the example of learning the skill of walking to illustrate the growth of alpha elements, alpha function, and the alpha membrane, which allow the thinking used in walking to be done unconsciously (Bion, 1962, p. 80). The alpha membrane allows for selective repression, not only in doing physical tasks, but psychical tasks as well. Consciousness is then not over-encumbered because the needed thinking and feeling is being done unconsciously by dream function alpha, thereby freeing consciousness to attend to other tasks. This sophisticated unconscious, as I call it (probably equivalent to Freud's preconscious), is to be contrasted with unconsciousness due to primary repression and perhaps much of Freud's secondary repression, used to avoid psychic pain. The psychic growth made possible by mature parental alpha function, including in psychoanalysis, allows for the development of psychic skills. Previously unbearable emotional experience can only then be borne—but borne by sophisticated unconscious thinking and feeling after such psychic skills are developed by working through—that is, through psychical exercise. Such unconscious thinking and feeling can become conscious as needed, just as one can become conscious of walking if needed. Unless conscious thinking and feeling is required, the activity can be done unconsciously so as not to overburden consciousness, which may be needed for other tasks.

Returning to my own experience, I found that what was at first incomprehensible in reading Bion became, as time passed, increasingly comprehensible. Now, reflecting upon my psychic experience as a practising analyst, I can increasingly feel the emotionality underlying his at-first difficult texts. I have found that the experience of reading Bion can be almost embarrassingly intimate. His writings are personal letters to colleagues and fellow travellers in the practice of analysis—as yet unmet or unborn, now and in years hence. Bion took very seriously the task of communicating his emotional (psychical) experiences in the practice of analysis to other analytic practitioners, so that we could compare them with our own experiences and engage him in dialogue about the practice of analysis. He wrote that we analysts need theories and abstractions when we try to write and speak to one another about our work, partly because these experiences are so painful. Our theories and abstractions make the pain more bearable to us. He also wrote that if only one or two understood his writings, he would count himself lucky. Bion was very aware of how the ongoing use of "psychoanalese" could become lifeless and empty, crushing the vitality out of psychoanalysis in analysts and analysands alike. He warned that psychoanalysis might well not survive the psychoanalytic Establishment.

Another feature of Bion's technique, noticeable to me from early on, was something with which I was totally unfamiliar at that time and would not have thought of as an interpretation. This was his calling attention to what I call "the splits". He would note that I had talked about A, B, and C, for example, and that each was a different facet of the same experience viewed from different angles, vertices, or points of view. This helped me move between the paranoid–schizoid (PS) and depressive (D) positions. The effect was not only acknowledging the discovery of a realisation and conception (D), but of unsaturating the conception so that it was now available as a preconception (PS) awaiting the next discovery through another realisation (D). I recall features of a dream which illustrate his calling attention to different vertices. In one part of the dream I was swimming through cloudy and turbulent water, so that I could only vaguely make out shapes, colours, and motion. In another part I was situated at a high vista point. Here the atmosphere was still, and details of the expansive view were sharp and clear. Bion related this to my bringing together two views of emotional experience regarding some specific event that was evident at the time. I was usually surprised by such interpretations, though they were frequent; I found them so simple and yet integrating and useful. At times when he and I were not clear as to what, specifically and concretely, the different vertices of a dream or association were referring, he would ask for other associations that often yielded the needed information. He would say that his own questions eliciting associations were also interpretations to call attention to the questions.

I recall a particular session, probably within the first year of my analysis, in which he began an interpretation from something I had said, the link to which was clear at the time. The interpretation was in typical Kleinian part-object language. I was utterly outraged by such a meaningless bunch of jargon, but before I could express outrage and dismay, Bion went on to say something like, "I have no idea whether there is any truth in what I just said, nor what it would mean in more practical and concrete terms. But you may, so I mention it to you in case you have some knowledge of it." I was flabbergasted. The room seemed to literally brighten. I felt a rush of associations which were indeed emotionally alive, along with feelings of amazement, exhilaration, discovery, and hope. I knew this was the way that, in time, one might conduct an ongoing self-analysis. It also emphasised Bion's faith (F) in psychoanalysis and its aesthetic qualities, and his willingness to take a leap—a chance—in using the link we had developed. There were many such instances thereafter. I recall another moment that involved my not confirming an interpretation he had made by accessing the emotional experience he was calling to my attention. I was ready to let it go when he said, "I may be the sort of thing you experienced with an aunt." In a flash, the emotional experience came into my awareness through a memory of just such an experience with an aunt. This is another example of his likely using his own psychoanalytic objects to successfully intuit mine.

Characteristic of Bion's technique was his use of questions. When I would mention things in conceptual terms (Rows D, E, F, and G), he would often ask if I were thinking of something specific. If I were not, he would frequently ask if I could think of something specific, adding, "The specific details may help me better understand your experience and give me some clue as to what to say." Here, I think, he was helping me search not only for my psychoanalytic objects, but for my associations to elicit his psychoanalytic objects that would hopefully closely correspond to mine. If successful, he would not only understand my emotional (psychical) experience, but perhaps be able to call attention to additional psychical or proto-psychical experiences, brought to life in me by his having utilised the emotions evoked in him via the specific details of my associations elicited by his questions.

A noteworthy set of experiences occurred on occasions when, not having grasped an interpretation, I would ask Bion if he could repeat it—to be met with his not uncommon response, "It is too late" or "too far by". A related dynamic would unfold if Bion, in turn, asked me what I had meant by some earlier remark, including his observation that it might be "too far by" for me to say. At first, I was dismayed and bemused by his comments that it was too late to repeat what he had said, and at times I felt he was deliberately withholding. But I now think, and at times even then suspected, that such remarks were due to his concept of the evanescent nature of psychoanalytic objects, especially when he needed access to his own psychoanalytic objects in order to make an alive interpretation. Instead of resorting to memory and desire, which he considered unsuited to psychic reality, he focused on that which can only be observed and described in the moment of its occurrence in analyst or analysand.

A recurring, even fairly frequent, feature of Bion's technique was the use of sarcasm, including facetious sarcasm, that sometimes shocked, stunned, frightened, and confused me, and to which I never really acclimatised. I did, in time, get tougher and more resilient in response to it. An example would be my commenting on his sounding sarcastic or facetious, and his responding that I was "perspicacious", which response also felt sarcastic to me. Was he responding to some sarcasm or aggression in me of which I was unaware? That question is still open.

In comparison with what I had learned in my classical American training, another innovative class of interpretation was what I refer to as Column 6 interpretations. A straightforward example of a Column 6 interpretation would be an analysand complaining of chest pain in himself or a loved one, evoking a psychoanalytic object (emotional experience) in the analyst. For instance, the analyst might have thoughts about calling an ambulance or getting himself or a loved one to the nearest hospital emergency room. Such a psychic object in the analyst might result in an interpretation that the analysand may have the idea of calling an ambulance or getting a loved one to the nearest hospital emergency room. This form of interpretation can easily sound like advice to the analysand; it is not meant as advice but calls attention to a state of mind enabling the analysand, seemingly oblivious to the possible urgency of the situation, to consider or reject taking an action. The analysand is then presented with an option that was previously unavailable. I am not certain how often such interpretations are made by more classical Kleinian analysts. I do know interpretations addressing projective identification in A6 with + and −(L, H, K) links are characteristic of classical Kleinian interpretations.

Bion's work with me and my subsequent study and understanding of Column 6 in Rows B and beyond (B though H) with K links, and probably L and H links, enable me to make such interpretations. These interpretations facilitate the "language of achievement", the type of psychical (emotional and ideational) experience (feeling and thinking) which leads to thoughtful decisions and actions in both the internal and external worlds. Bion describes the particular senses of loneliness, responsibility, and concern, including concern about whether one may be acting out by giving advice instead of interpreting, or whether the analysand will misconstrue such interpretations as advice. I found that my classical Freudian training did not provide models useful to me for making precisely these facilitating interpretations. This inability in particular contributed to my earlier sense of dissatisfaction with my practice of analysis. The omission of these interpretations at a propitious time deprives analysands of access to their language of achievement, the emotional experience needed in order to make useful changes in their lives externally and internally. I think Column 6 interpretations facilitate K to O transformations—to become (indeed, to be) one's self.

Yet another technical observation made by Bion was that reactive aggression due to the absence of needed alpha function, with the resultant hypertrophied projective identification, needs to be clearly differentiated from the envy aroused by the presence of needed alpha function supplied by the analyst (mature parental couple). Bion further developed Klein's model of mind in his differentiation of various component voices in the ensemble of internal objects and parts of self, regarding the same psychical object (envy, for example). Each component voice needs to be discretely felt by the analysand so that each voice can be individually and distinctly dealt with by the mature internal parents. This allows selective choices as to which voices are heeded for choosing specific action, whether wholesome gratification and/or constraint—the outcome of the language of achievement leading to and including Column 6 experience.

One final observation unique to Bion's perspective was that being without memory and desire is especially useful in spotting transformations in hallucinosis and unconscious hallucinations resulting from unbearable psychic pain and pathogenic projective identification. The latter produces psychic "leaks" that can be stopped if the analyst is able to spot them and provide the needed alpha function. If the analysand introjects this capacity, he or she then has an opportunity to develop the needed alpha function, to "plug the leak", and to develop psychic capacity instead.

I hope this description of my personal experience with Bion may help to clarify certain aspects in his writings as you come across them in your psychoanalytic sojourn.

Reference

Bion, W. R. (1962). *Learning from Experience*. New York: Basic Books.

CHAPTER 8

Bion and binocular vision*

Albert Mason

The author describes his contact with Bion over a twenty-year period, from Bion's supervision of his control case in London in 1960 to the period from 1968 to 1978 when they were both working in Los Angeles. He outlines Bion's views on the use of "instinct" and intuition in patient observation, the depressive position in patient and analyst, and memory and desire as impediments to knowledge of "ultimate reality". Some case material is presented, illustrating how Bion's ideas, particularly concerning attacks on linking, informed the course of the treatment. The author then discusses Freud's, Klein's, and Bion's approaches to the problem of resistance, Bion's expansion of some of Klein's ideas, his definitions of psychosis and his formulation concerning thoughts that develop before thinking. The author then argues how essential

---

* This paper is based on a presentation given at the 41st Congress of the International Psychoanalytical Association, Santiago, Chile, 1999. The paper was first published in 2000 in the *International Journal of Psychoanalysis 81*(5): 983–988, copyright © Institute of Psychoanalysis reprinted by permission of Taylor & Francis Ltd, http://www.tandfonline.com on behalf of Institute of Psychoanalysis.

it is for the analyst to differentiate between primitive projections from the patient that are pre-verbal attempts to communicate a state of mind and those that are an expression of hostility or control. He then discusses the importance of understanding idealising projections and differentiating these from a healthy positive transference. He concludes by characterising Bion's way of working in terms of his humility, his courage, and, fundamentally, his use of his intuitive binocular mind.

* * *

During the twenty years' contact I had with Wilfred Bion, first as a supervisee and later as a colleague, he said many things that have remained in my mind, much like the poems of my childhood. I believe this is because like poetry, they were loaded with meaning at many different levels. This paper is an attempt to verbalise how these meanings affected me. My very first contact with Bion was in London in 1960 when he supervised one of my control cases. To my great surprise the patient in question, a young man of twenty-three, began his analysis by going directly to the couch, lying down, and saying without preamble: "I woke up in the middle of the night, got out of bed, and switched on the light to see if I … was in bed or not." With some trepidation, knowing what would be considered unsuitable for a control case, I repeated the patient's first sentence to Dr Bion. He stroked his moustache reflectively, and with a perfectly straight face said, "Well, we are all entitled to a second opinion."

My very last contact with Bion was in Los Angeles in 1979, one warm evening sitting on the patio outside my house. We were both a little sad as it was the end of his California adventure, and while he wanted to return to England to be with his children, he was also leaving behind many friends. He was watching one of my cats clean its whiskers with precise, beautiful strokes. "You know," he said, "if someone were to build a machine that could catch mice and also keep itself clean, it would cost a lot of money!"

It would be very easy to dismiss either of these comments as merely examples of Bion's wry sense of humour, but this would be a monocular view of a binocular man. Not only was Bion binocular, but his ideas concerning multiple vertices show that he was trinocular, quatrocular—and so on. In addition to sensory experience, Bion drew our attention to the non-sensory use of "instinct" and intuition in the observation of the patient. He always emphasised that the more points of view we have, the firmer our sense of conviction about our observations. These points of view should be allowed to emerge "patiently", with a mind approximating to what Klein called the paranoid–schizoid position; that is, a mind that is unintegrated; a mind that experiences "O" (ultimate reality); or becomes "O" through knowledge gained by experience. Bion regarded the evolution of understanding as a helpful idea but not quite the same as becoming "O", whose presence is felt and recognised but cannot be known. He was convinced that despite the most careful gathering of information, which he would call the "luxury of evidence", there would always remain the indescribable, the ineffable, the "O".

Bion also said that following an effective interpretation, both patient and analyst felt sad. This he believed implied the patient's achievement of the depressive position of Klein, and Bion's binocular view was that the depressive experience was also felt by the analyst. Feelings of sadness associated with separation and loss were the inevitable consequence of an effective interpretation and would always be mutual, however gratifying the analytic progress might be.

What Bion was clear about is that both memory and desire, the past and future tense of an event, are impediments to knowing the ultimate reality. The state of mind he considered necessary he described as "faith" and he went to some lengths to assure us that, for him, the word had no religious meaning. He liked Freud's comment about blinding oneself artificially and linked that state to the absence of memory and desire—a piercing shaft of darkness. In this darkness one can "see", "hear", and "feel" the mental phenomena whose reality, according to Bion, no practising psychoanalyst has any doubt about.

When Bion said, "we are all entitled to a second opinion", he was talking about the different views the patient needs of himself. Initially, the patient referred to earlier was coming for my opinion in addition to his own. However, his first act was to throw his own light on himself, showing that in phantasy he and I were narcissistically commingled. The patient was already identified with the analyst as light-thrower and presumably then my opinion would be his own. Bion also meant by his comment that, like the patient, we all need an object relationship, not just a narcissistic involvement. It is not just a second opinion we are entitled to, but a separate life. This is the struggle we are always engaged in externally with our objects, and internally with ourselves.

I believe that this theme was being restated from another vector in the cat incident. Here. Bion was drawing my attention to the priceless quality of life, and how in vain we try to replace the living with material and mechanical substitutes—what one of my patients calls "stuff". The content of this statement during one of his last evenings in California— and in fact the last time I was to see him—was particularly poignant. It reiterated for me why we try to build and become those things called machines, which are always "new and improved" (an ironic title of one of Bion's lectures) and totally replaceable, unlike the irreplaceable living being who may leave us and whom we inevitably have to lose.

Bion's ideas, like those of Freud and Klein, seem to penetrate one's vision, and I find that my view of patients—like the complex view from the fly's multifaceted eye—has a Bion window that permanently affects the way I see human behaviour. Bion once told me about a patient who remarked: "You said such and such last week," to which he replied in a confrontational manner: "I've forgotten what I said last week!"

I think he was trying to convey the need to experience meaning at that precise moment and to show that no experience is ever quite the same and cannot be re-experienced or reconstructed exactly. Living experience is not recoverable because life is ever-changing. The denuda-tion of the object's living quality is an attempt to deny loss and death by substituting a dead thing for a living object and calling it equiva-lent or better. The bottle is preferred to the breast and the breast to the whole human being. Masturbation or narcissism is chosen before object-relatedness for it is believed to be predictable and safe, whereas life, as Bion frequently said, "is full of surprises—most of them unpleas-ant!" Only a machine can replicate an event precisely. The patient who was asking Bion to recall the previous session was enacting a repetition compulsion to deny the passage of time and its inevitable losses.

A patient of mine dreamed that he was *joining an electric wire to a water pipe to make a jagger*. He had no associations to the dream and did not know what a "jagger" was. My own association was to Mick Jagger, the rock star, and to his obscene posturing. Bion's work on linkages reminded me that the link the patient was envisaging was inappropriate, dangerous and, by my association, ugly. I inferred that this link was his envious and devalued view of his parental intercourse, and also what he felt were my attempts to conduct an analysis rendered futile. Since his envy also contained his admiration and the wish to emulate, he projectively identified with this phantasised link. Thus, his thinking and thoughts became inappropriate, obscene, explosive, and often senseless. This was a link I could not have made without Bion's teaching.

A playwright I treated made audiences roar with laughter at his inappropriate non sequiturs. He was tortured with obsessional thoughts about every woman he saw or passed on the street. These thoughts were largely connected to doubts about whether or not he had had a sexual relationship with the women. He was also tormented by thoughts about his wife and children: was his wife consistently unfaithful? And were the children his own? His analysis revealed that he found it impossible to believe that his mother would allow his father to perform such a disgraceful act as having intercourse with her. He was also convinced, despite his strong resemblance to his father, that he was adopted. His phantasy about his parents' sex was that it was either non-existent or that it was disgusting. Likewise, I as his analyst either did nothing of value, or made dirty allusions to him of which I should be ashamed. His bizarre and inappropriate mental links identified in every way with his phantasies about his parents' intercourse, which he imagined occurring in every possible perverse and abnormal way.

Equating the attacked and distorted phantasies about the parents' sexual activities with the patient's thought disorder was a link commensurate with Bion's binocular view of linkages, and the attacks they provoke. The idea that envious and jealous projections occur when a child devalues adult capacities and functions, and then identifies with the damaged object or part object is a simple enough idea, once one gets the hang of it. Freud saw this when he described how stools could be equated with babies or penises. But to equate devalued parental intercourse with thought disorders was a stroke of genius—a splendid link that Bion made for us, and one that has affected and helped the understanding and treatment of psychosis greatly.

The unconscious is unconscious because it contains feelings, impulses, and aspects of our personality that we do not wish to be

conscious of. It follows then that any attempt to make what is unconscious conscious will be resisted. The art of helping the patient to admit
back into consciousness that which he or she has repressed or split off is
the most difficult aspect of what has been called "the impossible profes-
sion", and Freud, Klein, and Bion all addressed different aspects of this
problem.

Freud explored our infantile sexual fantasies and wishes and showed
how the forbidden, conflictual, and painful aspects of these fantasies
led to their repression. He focused a great deal on the understanding
of jealousy. Klein enriched our understanding about infantile hostility,
cruelty, and other aspects of our destructiveness that were split off and
projected because of the guilt and shame they caused us. She threw particular light on a form of hostility she called envy and showed us how, in
addition to frustration and deprivation, gratification could also produce
spite and hostility. Both excessive jealousy or envy, or a combination of
them, can cause more than resistance, namely a phenomenon we call a
negative therapeutic reaction—a form of resistance that is extreme and
sometimes intractable.

Bion added another idea to those of Freud and Klein, which is illustrated by a patient of mine who had the following dream. "*I was riding a
motorcycle in a rut in the road. There were many chicks which ran across
the rut and were squashed.*" Associations too elaborate to recount here
led me to interpret that the chicks stood for the patient's sister who was
four years younger than the patient. Bion's formulation that "the patient
attacks an interpretation as though it were a sibling" gave me an important understanding about the patient's resistances and general failure to
fulfil his potential in life (caught in a rut). It was not only the new baby
(chick, sister, interpretation) that was attacked and resisted, but any
"new" information that could add something to the patient's life. This
formulation of Bion's adds to our understanding of the Oedipus myth
where the father, Laius, attempts to kill the new baby, which he phanta-
sises threatens his life and possessions. It also enriches our understanding of the whole concept of infantile omnipotence and omniscience,
which is a state of mind where nothing new can be accepted, as all is
already known. The idea that anything new stands for a sibling, who
also represents the result of the creative intercourse of the parents, certainly enlarges our understanding about why an interpretation can be

resisted to the death, for it is felt, like Oedipus, to threaten the life of the existing state—called "Laius".

If we apply these ideas socially, we need the right combination of chaos and order for creativity to flourish. New ideas are frustrated if societies are not receptive to the chaos that comes from change, yet an appropriate degree of order is necessary to take advantage of creative breakthroughs. Great creativity requires hard facts, wild imagination, and non-logical leaps forward that are proved to be right by working backwards to known principles. Only the rebellious and the truly courageous can do it.

Klein suggested two ideas: (1) that the baby did not experience hunger as the absence of a good breast, but the presence of a bad breast to be evacuated; and (2) that anxiety was a necessary spur to development. Bion explored these ideas separately and together, binocularly. He defined psychosis, for example, as the choice of evasion of pain rather than the pursuit of pleasure. He further defined serious mental illness as the evasion of frustration rather than the modification of it. He also had the idea of the "no breast" as the place where a thought, which could lead to thinking, occurred. It was not only psychosis that was illuminated by these concepts, but, as Bion said, "No analysis is complete without the analysis of the psychotic part of all patients' personalities." These two ideas, building on each other, illuminate the work we do with all patients. I still find that the persecutor "presence of the absence"— both Klein's and Bion's view of our response to frustration—is a most evocative and powerful concept.

Another important example of Bion's binocular vision is his formulation that thoughts develop before thinking, and that the first thought is a no-thing, which is the preconception of a breast when it is absent and desired. This proto-thought is fit only for projection (beta element), and if the breast (maternal object) is available and capable of accepting this projection because it is capable of a state Bion called reverie, the breast then provides what the patient needs, introjects and takes over as his own apparatus (alpha function). The patient can then contain what was previously uncontainable and transform these proto-thoughts into thoughts that he can think and understand (alpha elements). Presumably one aspect of these primitive elements would be our predator instinct, a primitive aggressivity, which is felt to threaten the patient from within, and thus needs to be projected. Money-Kyrle believed that the external projection of this predator instinct produced a paranoia that was needed for survival. If we did not fear the tiger, for instance, our survival would be short-lived. An obese patient dreamed about *a pit filled with lions and tigers that he had to feed in order to pass*. Here we see a clear example in which the absence of food is felt to be the presence of a dangerous object. Understanding and interpreting the underlying phantasy diminishes the unconscious anxiety of these primitive elements.

The analyst's understanding that these primitive projections are due to desperation rather than hostility is a significant technical consideration, and while it is important to interpret the hostile nature of the patient's projections when appropriate, it is also vital to understand that at times the projections are desperate and are primitive communications of persecutory states. The analyst's capacity to contain these, and not see or interpret them as hostility is vital for the patient to experience, for the patient can then identify with this capacity, eventually contain the projections himself or herself, and finally understand and modify the overwhelming nature of the primitive anxiety. If these communicative projections are interpreted as hostility, the patient will then experience the analyst as also being unable to contain them, which is not only unhelpful but dangerous, as the persecution increases and may lead to action as the only available source of relief.

An example of such a situation occurred when a patient of mine brought a large carving knife to her session and proceeded to demonstrate rather enthusiastically how well she could fence and how extensive was her knowledge of the male anatomy. Interpretations of hostility and triumph increased her violence and my fear. It was only when I interpreted her wish to project into me her fear of being murdered that she stopped, lay down on the couch and proceeded to tell me her fears of being murdered, of many years' duration. This eventually led to an exploration of her suicidal tendencies and suicidal attempts, which had not, in fact, emerged clearly until that moment.

It is also important for the analyst to be able to contain and to understand (or detoxify) projections of an idealising nature. These, at times, may be even more difficult to deal with than projections of a hating nature, as the analyst may feel gratified by them and believe that at last someone understands and appreciates how wonderful he or she really is. A loving *folie à deux* may then occur with the unfortunate consequences of unconscious persecutory anxiety remaining unanalysed or an acting out between patient and analyst who become friends or lovers.

One of Bion's most interesting observations was that there are only about half a dozen different interpretations, but that the details are always different. He used and taught several models like container-contained, and PS ↔ D, but always insisted that one had to forget them during work, as the details of these models for each patient would be totally different. When he talked about the absence of memory or desire, he was saying something like, "Each session is new, and one must forget that the patient on the couch is married with two children, for today he or she might be single." The same theme is echoed in the cat incident; living things are irreplaceable and unique. They even differ from themselves from day to day, and sometimes from moment to moment.

Bion once told me that he thought swimming was not really exercise as it was effortless. This I think is a good description of how he worked. Effort is memory or desire—the work we feel we have to do against resistance; but Bion's reverie was a description of him swimming—letting his unconscious do the work while he floated into becoming "O". I would hasten to add that Bion's "effortless" swimming was possible only because of the long years of training he had undergone to acquire this skill.

Bion was particularly sensitive to the vicissitudes of omnipotence and always drew attention to its cruelty, just as the Scriptures tell us that everlasting damnation is the punishment for sin. His own attitude and work were always humble; for instance, he would talk about an interpretation as a "sighting shot"—a term taken from gunnery. This was the antithesis of the concept of a "correct" interpretation. Like Klein, who worked by "serial approximations", Bion's "sighting shot" was a trial effort that usually needed some adjustment. In a way it was linked to his "making the best of a bad job", which is what I believe he felt patients failed to do, analysts needed to do, and finally, what contentment in life was all about. He was always amused by the idea of "new and improved", that universal label we give to cars, detergents, and analytic theories when we wish to sell them. He clearly believed that there was precious little new and doubted if much had improved except propaganda.

I recall that following a lengthy and flattering introduction of Bion at one of his public lectures, he remarked: "After listening to all those wonderful things about myself, I can hardly wait to hear what I have to say." While this was half humorous, I also knew it was totally true. He never knew exactly what he was going to say. He may have repeated his themes, but the details were always different. At times his lectures were brilliant, and at times not, but they were never remotely the same, and I am quite certain he often surprised himself as well as the audience. Like a technically superb musician, he could now improvise, and the cadenzas and embellishments would always be a little different.

I remember Bion saying with a slightly dangerous glint in his eye: "They say … [I will leave you to guess whom he meant by 'they'] … that I am psychotic. Well, that may be so, but I am not insane!" When one aligns this with yet another binocular statement of his: "One is just as likely to be shot in the back running away from the enemy as one is to be killed advancing towards him," it gives us a powerful view of a powerful man. It is clear that he was not going to run away or evade any dangerous confrontation, whether it was the attacks of others, living in a new country at the age of seventy, an internal doubt or conflict, the most disturbed patient, or the most disturbing idea. Facing the enemy won him many decorations for valour in the real war. In a similar manner, he never shied away from the dangerous confrontation of primitive thoughts and madness, whether they arose from outside or inside.

I well remember the clarity Rosenfeld brought to my confusion when treating a psychotic, and the confusion Bion brought to my clarity under similar conditions—lest I grow too smug and not notice landmines, or fail to "think when the bombs were dropping". Bion said that no analysis can be conducted by one analyst alone, which was another way of stating that we all need those extra internal eyes to supervise us when we are caught up in projections—ours and the patient's. This binocular vision frees us to take part in a scene in someone else's play without losing ourselves. Here we need more than two eyes; we need at least two minds.

I have often likened analysis to riding a bicycle. Recalling the process, I first had to learn to hold the handlebars and use the brakes, then to balance, and to learn all the rules of the road. When these were mastered, Paula Heimann told me to take my hands off the handlebars and let my countertransference take over. Finally, Bion removed the front wheel and told me to steer with that intuitive binocular mind, which I hoped was a distillate of all I had learned and had now forgotten. While it appears to have no memory or desire, the binocular mind has digested its experiences and now faces the unknown enemy outside in the patient, as well as the saboteur within itself.

Index